true woman 101

divine design

true woman 101

divine design

an eight-week study on biblical womanhood

Mary A. Kassian

Nancy Leigh DeMoss

MOODY PUBLISHERS

CHICAGO

All Scripture quotations, unless otherwise indicated, are taken from *The Holy
Bible, English Standard Version.* Copyright © 2000, 2001 by Crossway Bibles, a
division of Good News Publishers. Used by permission. All rights reserved.

Scripture quotations marked NIV are taken from the *Holy Bible,
New International Version®*, NIV®. Copyright © 1973, 1978, 1984 by
Biblica, Inc.™ Used by permission of Zondervan. All rights reserved
worldwide. www.zondervan.com

Scripture quotations marked NKJV are taken from the *New King James Version*.
Copyright © 1982 by Thomas Nelson, Inc. Used by permission.
All rights reserved.

Scripture quotations marked HCSB are taken from the *Holman Christian Standard
Bible®*, Copyright © 1999, 2000, 2002, 2003 by Holman Bible Publishers. Used
by permission. Holman Christian Standard Bible®, Holman CSB®, and HCSB® are
federally registered trademarks of Holman Bible Publishers.

Emphasis to Scripture has been added by the authors.

Cover Design: Laura Shaffer/Revive Our Hearts
Interior Design: Julia Ryan | www.DesignByJulia.com
Cover Image: Getty Images
Embellishments: Shutterstock/Danussa
Interior Images: Shutterstock, Fotolio, iStock
Authors Photos: Photography by Katie

Library of Congress Cataloging-in-Publication Data

Kassian, Mary A.
True woman 101 : divine design : an eight week study on biblical womanhood
/ Mary A. Kassian, Nancy Leigh DeMoss.
p. cm.
Includes bibliographical references.
ISBN 978-0-8024-0356-8
1. Women--Religious aspects--Christianity--Textbooks. I. DeMoss, Nancy
Leigh. II. Title.
BT704.K38 2012
248.8'43071--dc23
2011047748

We hope you enjoy this book from Moody Publishers. Our goal is to
provide high-quality, thought-provoking books and products that connect
truth to your real needs and challenges. For more information on other books
and products written and produced from a biblical perspective,
go to www.moodypublishers.com or write to:

Moody Publishers
820 N. LaSalle Boulevard
Chicago, IL 60610

3 5 7 9 10 8 6 4

Printed in the United States of America

With heartfelt gratitude

for our dear "band of praying sisters"—
Carolyn, Dannah, Holly, Jennifer, Kim, and Mary Ann

You are true women of God.
Your prayers, encouragement, insight, courage,
and friendship have put wind in our sails.
Thank you for your partnership
in birthing and advancing the
True Woman movement.
We are believing God with you
for a mighty outpouring of His Spirit
in and through the hearts of women in our day.

"*True Woman 101: Divine Design* lays a beautiful and thorough biblical foundation for the topic of biblical womanhood. I highly recommend it for any woman serious about displaying the glory of God in her distinctive role as a woman."

Mary Delk

Minister for Women, Bethlehem Baptist Church (Minneapolis, MN)

"A must-use resource for every congregation in North America. In a culture where diversity is celebrated, the beautiful diversity of biblical manhood and womanhood has been marred and discredited. My dear friends Mary and Nancy reclaim the true picture of God and His love for humanity as seen in His design for our womanhood!"

Dannah Gresh

Bestselling author and founder, Pure Freedom

"One of the best compliments a woman can receive is 'She feels comfortable in her own skin.' I want to be that woman, don't you? If you do, then *True Woman 101* will help you become her! As you learn about and embrace God's design, you'll get a dramatic makeover from the inside out and will transform your womanhood into something you're far more than just 'comfortable' with; something worth celebrating!"

Jennifer Rothschild

Author, founder WomensMinistry.net and Fresh Grounded Faith Events

"The Lord has given Mary and Nancy a message for women that clearly defines womanhood, how she should live, and what purpose God has designed her to fulfill. If you are a woman anywhere between 18 and 108 this book has a specific and personal message for you!"

Debbie Stuart

Director of Women's Ministry, Prestonwood Baptist Church (Plano, TX)

"Identity definition and design—God's design—are increasingly minimized if not ignored. We are building a legacy of gender competition and confusion. But God has called us to embrace and celebrate who He created us to be. That's why this resource is such a timely, wonderful gift. This eight-part study will refresh and encourage your heart. This is liberating stuff!"

Dr. Crawford and Karen Loritts

Authors, speakers; (Crawford) Senior Pastor, Fellowship Bible Church (Roswell, GA)

"Knowing how God has uniquely created women is key to the decisions I make in almost every area of my life. I am so thankful that the Lord has equipped Nancy and Mary to bring to life the timeless truths of Scripture 'for such a time as this.' If you are desperate to know how God's design is meant to play out in your choices, don't pass up this treasure!"

Dr. Juli Slattery

Author, family psychologist, cohost for *Focus on the Family*

"*True Woman 101* is a discipleship resource that combines biblical principles of womanhood with practical applications. The daily readings make you feel as if you are sitting at your kitchen table having coffee with Mary and Nancy. These Titus 2 women take us to the grace of the gospel. They show us Jesus, the One who transforms us into true women."

Susan Hunt

Author, speaker, Women's Ministry Consultant for PCA Christian Education Publications

"*True Woman 101* gives women what they chiefly need—an extreme makeover of the interior not the exterior! I appreciate the thorough content which drives home the message that true womanhood is about emanating the beauty and grace of Jesus Christ for the glory of God. When a coalition of humble, intentional women begin to radiate from the inside out, the world will sit up and take notice that the gospel isn't phony, it's the real deal."

Leslie Bennett

Director of Women's Ministries, Northeast Presbyterian Church, PCA (Columbia, SC)

"The True Woman study provides something every modern woman needs: a wake-up call and practical help to live life as a woman of God, rather than (without realizing it) as a woman of the culture."

Shaunti Feldhahn

Author, speaker, columnist

contents

overview of lessons

"The greatest influence on earth whether for good or for evil, is possessed by woman."
—ADOLPHE MONOD

Designer handbags, designer fashions, designer frames, designer décor …a lot of women gravitate toward designer brands because they're high quality. They're often especially exquisite. They're authentic. They're true to the designer's precise specifications.

Did you know that God has a divine design for womanhood? And His plan is spectacular—far more attractive than the cheap, fake imitations the world promotes!

The women's movement rejected the idea that God has a divine design for womanhood. It proposed that it was up to women to decide what womanhood was all about. It taught us to believe that our lives—and the choices we make—are all about us. It led us to think that the differences between male and female aren't all that important —that we can arbitrarily choose our roles, and determine the meaning of gender. It encouraged us to adopt a new, feminist-inspired design.

The current cultural ideal for womanhood encourages women to be strident, sexual, self-centered, independent, and—above all—powerful and in control. But sadly, this model of womanhood hasn't delivered the happiness and fulfillment it promised.

We have both been actively involved in ministering to women for more than thirty years and have seen this sadness and disappointment in spades. Again and again, we have witnessed the emotional and relational wreckage of hearts and homes that have gone with the flow and bought into our culture's view of what it means to be a woman. We have received countless letters and emails and looked into the eyes of thousands of women who feel the deep pain of unfulfilled expectations.

In many cases, this dysfunction is the unavoidable consequence of living in a fallen world. But far too often, it's apparent that we are seeing the fallout of widespread confusion and faulty beliefs about a woman's design and mission.

You see, the Bible teaches that it's not up to us to decide what womanhood is all about. It says that God created male and female for a vital, specific purpose. His design isn't arbitrary, unimportant, or expendable.

Your womanhood is not a biological accident. It's not a matter of chance. God was intentional when He made you a woman. And He wants you to discover, embrace, and delight in the beauty of His spectacular design. He wants you to enjoy something so much more valuable than the world's cheap imitations and knockoffs. He wants you to be a True Woman!

What exactly is a True Woman? She is, quite simply, a woman who is being molded and shaped according to

> "It is time for women of biblical faith to reclaim our territory. We know the Designer. We have His instruction manual. If we don't display the Divine design of His female creation, no one will. But if we do, it will be a profound testimony to a watching, needy world."[1]
>
> **Susan Hunt**

God's design. She's a woman who loves Jesus and whose life is grounded in, tethered to, and enabled by Christ and His gospel. As a result, she is serious about bringing her thoughts and actions in line with what the Bible says about who she is and how she ought to live. She is a woman who rejects the world's pattern for womanhood, and gladly wears God's designer label instead.

the true woman movement

Years ago, the Lord began to put on each of our hearts a burden for a new women's movement—a countercultural revolution, in which women would reject the world's model of womanhood, and would joyfully follow Christ and embrace His design.[2] When our paths finally intersected and we discovered our common burden, we began to seek the Lord together about how to share that vision with other women.

Long story short, in October 2008, over 6,000 women from forty-eight states and seven countries gathered in Chicago for the first True Woman conference, hosted by *Revive Our Hearts* along with other ministry partners. The goal of that event was to help women . . .

- *Discover and embrace* God's design and mission for their lives
- *Reflect the beauty* and heart of Jesus Christ to their world
- *Intentionally pass* the baton of Truth on to the next generation
- *Pray earnestly* for an outpouring of God's Spirit in their families, churches, nation, and world

Since that initial launch, thousands of women have attended subsequent True Woman conferences. Thousands more from scores of countries around the world have signed the True Woman Manifesto, are following the True Woman blog, and/or are interacting with other women through various True Woman social media communities. True Woman events, small groups, and studies have spontaneously sprung up all across the country.

What a joy it is to see True Woman becoming a grassroots movement—not only in the U.S. but in other countries around the world—through which Christ is being put on display in a greater way through women's lives!

This True Woman Bible study is a response to the many requests we have received for further biblical teaching and practical resources. It contains essential, foundational teaching on what the Bible says womanhood is all about. That's why we've called it *True Woman 101*.

The eight weeks in this study are each divided into five lessons—it should take you approximately twenty minutes to complete each lesson. To get the most out of this study, we'd suggest you go through

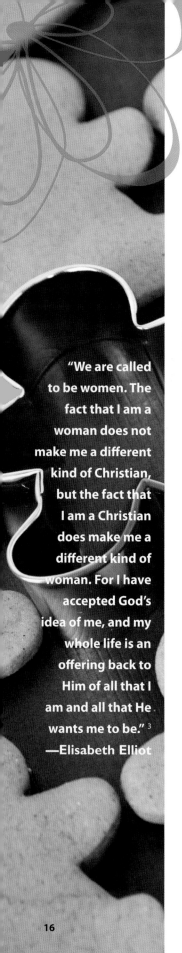

it with a group of friends. At the end of each week, we've provided some questions to help you discuss what you've read and further explore and apply the Bible's teachings on womanhood. When you're done, encourage your friends to start their own groups. You'll find many additional resources, including companion videos and helps for group leaders, at www.truewoman101.com.

Decades ago, the women's movement set out to spread its radical message and vision through small groups that met, multiplied, and eventually ignited a revolution. Our desire is that a new revolution will take root and spread in our day, as Christian women band together to ask, "How can we more fully reflect the beauty and gospel of Christ to our world, through the expression of our true, biblical design?"

beyond caricatures and cookie cutters

The Bible presents a design for True Womanhood that applies to *all* women— at any age and at any stage of life—old, young; single, married, divorced, widowed; with children or without, whatever. Its design applies to women of every personality type, every educational level, every career track, every socioeconomic status, and every culture. God's design transcends social customs, time, and circumstance.

In this study, we have tried to focus on timeless biblical principles rather than the specific application of those principles. We wanted to provide a resource with foundational teaching that could be applied to different stages and circumstances of life, and that would be just as applicable to the great-granddaughters of our generation as it is to us.

When it comes to womanhood, most of us have been exposed to clichéd advice, shallow caricatures, and cookie-cutter solutions. It is our hope that this resource will shift the discussion to a better focus. We pray that it will

- enable you to explore God's timeless design for womanhood straight from His Word
- help you wrestle with how to apply God's design to your season of life
- encourage you to have grace toward women who differ in life circumstance and application
- equip you to pass on the message of True Womanhood to the next generation

Caricatures and cookie-cutter patterns won't do. God's design for womanhood is much broader and more glorious than that.

Discovering and living out the meaning of True Womanhood will be a journey for you, as it has been (and is) for us. At points, you may find yourself disagreeing with what you're reading, or struggling with some of the implications of this teaching. We've had some of those same reactions ourselves! We would simply encourage you to turn to God's Word with an open, seeking heart. Ask His Spirit to teach you, to give you understanding, and to incline your heart to say "Yes, Lord!" to His Word and His ways.

a divine design!

"*Why can't a woman be more like a man?*" That's the question famously posed by Professor Henry Higgins in the classic musical *My Fair Lady*. It's a good question. Why *can't* a woman be more like a man? Why can't a man be more like a woman? What does it mean to be a woman? What does it mean to be a man? What's the difference? And does it really matter?

The Bible's answer to the professor's question is that God doesn't want His daughters to be more like men. Nor does He want His sons to be more like women. God created male and female. He isn't interested in blurring or obliterating gender—He's interested in redeeming it. His divine design reflects profound truths about God's character and about the gospel. He wants us to discover the beauty of His plan for manhood and womanhood, and to experience the joy and fulfillment of being exactly who He created us to be.

That's the reason for this study. And that's our hope and prayer for you. Whatever your season of life, whatever your current challenges or circumstances, may you glorify God and make the gospel believable to those around you, as you reflect His divine design and become His True Woman!

Mary Nancy

"I believe the time is ripe for a new movement— a seismic holy quake of countercultural men and women who dare to take God at His Word— men and women whose hearts are broken over the gender confusion and spiritual/emotional/ relational carnage of our day, and who have the courage to believe and delight in God's plan for male and female."

—Mary A. Kassian

gender matters

Most of us have learned (the hard way?!) that you need to follow the manufacturer's instructions, if you want to put things together right. Recently I (Mary) bought and assembled a large wall unit for my husband's office. It was packaged in about a dozen boxes and contained hundreds of pieces of hardware.

I followed the directions step-by-step. Each piece had a specific purpose that became apparent as the unit came together. The process was complex and took several hours. I made some mistakes, and had to go back and pore over the pattern a few times, but I finally got it put together right. And it looks beautiful!

I'm so glad the manufacturer of that wall unit included instructions. The designer of a product is the one who knows that product best. The manufacturer is the one who knows why and how it's made, how to put it together, and how it's supposed to work.

The same principle applies to our lives. Our Creator knows us best. He's the one who knows how and why He created us male and female. As the Designer, He knows the proper way to order and fit together our lives and relationships—according to their intended design.

Jesus was once confronted with a question about male-female relationships. The Pharisees wanted to discuss cultural customs and practices about divorce, and have Jesus endorse one of two popular views (Matt. 19:3–9). But Jesus took the discussion to an entirely different level.

Jesus indicated that in order to get their thinking right, they needed to look beyond all their cultural customs and social conventions, as well as the distortions that had been introduced by sin. They couldn't hope to get things right by arguing over personal opinions or a list of human "dos" and "don'ts."

In order to think and behave correctly, they needed to understand God's original and highest intention for man and woman. And to do this, they needed to look back to creation—to God's pattern—to understand the intent of His original design.

It isn't possible to understand the Bible's teaching on men and women without first understanding God's purpose in creating them. So that's where we're going to start. We're going to lay the foundation of True Womanhood by going back to the first few chapters of Genesis. We'll have a look at what God had in mind, and what things were like between man and woman in the paradise of Eden, before sin marred our relationships.

As you walk through this week's lessons, try to do what Jesus challenged the Pharisees to do. First, look beyond the customs, social conventions, and distortions of male and female of which you are no doubt painfully aware. Second, remember that God's original design for male and female is good. In fact, God's assessment is that it's better than good . . . it's *very* good (Gen. 1:31)!

Regardless of what you may have been told by our culture, regardless of the pain you may have experienced due to the brokenness and twisting of sin, His plan for womanhood—and His plan for you—is beautiful and it is good!

As we look into the Designer's manual together, we think you'll see just how important your womanhood is, and how much gender really does matter!

As obvious as it may be that it's important to follow the designer's directions when it comes to assembling shelves, it's a point so many women (and men) miss when it comes to "assembling" their lives and relationships. The fact is, any time we fail to consult the Designer and follow the directions He has provided, we're going to end up with a mess!

Perhaps you relate—you've tried to build your life and relationships on your own, without the guidance of your Designer, and the result is chaos. Maybe it's time for you to go back and pore over the pattern to find out what your womanhood is all about.

The good news is that Jesus Christ can change you, rearrange the pieces of your life, and put things together the way He intended, so your life can become a thing of beauty and usefulness!

on display

"Then God said, 'Let us make man in our image, after our likeness. And let them have dominion over the fish of the sea and over the birds of the heavens and over the livestock and over all the earth and over every creeping thing that creeps on the earth.' So God created man in his own image, in the image of God he created him; male and female he created them."

Genesis 1:26–27

Have you ever found yourself pausing as you were on the verge of doing something really important? Last summer, I (Mary) sewed a dress for my son's wedding. I had checked all the measurements, made all the necessary adjustments, and carefully pinned the pattern pieces to the material. I picked up my scissors and positioned the sharp blades along the first cut line. But then, just before shearing the costly fabric, I took a deep breath and momentarily paused.

It's not that I was uncertain. I knew I had gotten everything right. It's just that I knew that my next action was significant in the pursuit of my goal — and the feeling caught my attention. I imagine it's a bit like the moment before a surgeon makes the first incision, or an artist lays hammer and chisel to an exquisite piece of marble, or a gemologist cuts the first facet of a weighty diamond.

In the first chapter of Genesis, we see the Creator reflectively pause before His final and greatest creative act—the language introducing this act ("Let us make man in our image") indicates an upcoming deliberative action with forethought. There was no question in God's mind about what He was going to do. No. He had settled on His plan long before the foundation of the world. It was already in motion. At His word, the galaxies and planets, the sun and moon had all been formed and aligned. The  earth had ripened with life: the ground had sprouted vegetation; the sky, sea, and land now teemed with every sort of living creature.

Everything was in place. Everything was ready. It all led up to this moment —and, as we will see, this moment pointed to another moment far off in time but eternally present in the mind of God. THE moment. The significance of what God was about to do was deeper and more profound than even the angels could fathom. He was about to make man—and to make him male and female.

Genesis 1:26–27 describes God's "reflective moment."
Read the verses in the margin and fill in the blanks of the diagram below.

GOD → **MAN**

In our _____

After our _____

Male Female

Who do you think the dialogue in Genesis 1:26 was between?
To whom does "us" and "our" refer?

_____

_____

_____

The discussion about creating man and woman took place among members of the Godhead. It may have been among all three: Father, Son, and Holy Spirit. But at the very least, it involved the Father and His Son, as Scripture draws parallels between that relationship and the relationship of the man and the woman (see 1 Cor. 11:3). We'll talk more about that later, but for now, just think about this: *When God created male and female, He had the dynamic of His own relationship in mind.*

The Lord created the two sexes to reflect something about God. He patterned the male-female relationship ("them") after the "us/our" relationship that exists within God. He designed the two sexes to put God on display.

Why do you think God created two different sexes, and not just one?

_____

_____

_____

_____

displaying His image

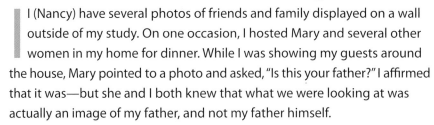

I (Nancy) have several photos of friends and family displayed on a wall outside of my study. On one occasion, I hosted Mary and several other women in my home for dinner. While I was showing my guests around the house, Mary pointed to a photo and asked, "Is this your father?" I affirmed that it was—but she and I both knew that what we were looking at was actually an image of my father, and not my father himself.

Just as the photo of my dad provides a snapshot of what he looked like, so mankind provides a glimpse of what God is like. Humans were the only creatures that God created "in His image" and "after His likeness."

The word "cloud" contains words closely associated with the concept of "image" and "likeness." Cross out the three words that do not belong:

> compare   model   correlate   mirror
> hide   reflect   imitate   picture   display
> represent   copy   shadow   emulate
> resemble   conceal   disregard

What are some ways you can think of that humans resemble/reflect the image of God?

_____

_____

Being created in God's image includes the ability to think and make moral choices. It means that we share in God's nature. Humans have personality; they have the capacity for creativity, truth, wisdom, love, holiness, and justice.

Scripture also indicates that being made in the image of God gives man capacity for spiritual fellowship with Him. What's more, it allows man to have dominion over the work of God's hands—to govern creation as God's representative.

How does the truth that mankind is created in the image of God speak to the chronic feelings of inferiority and worthlessness that many women experience?

The photo of my dad in my hallway puts my dad on display for everyone who comes into my house to see. Likewise, God want us to put Him on display, so that everyone who looks at us sees the beauty of His image. It's a profound honor and responsibility to bear the image of God.

Read Isaiah 43:6–7 in your Bible. For what purpose does God say He created "sons" and "daughters"?

Scripture teaches that womanhood isn't about prettying ourselves up and putting ourselves on display. Our purpose in life is to put God on display—to reflect His glory in ways we as women were uniquely created to do.

Do you feel that your womanhood displays God's glory? Explain why or why not.

→ **Close today's lesson by praying and asking** the Lord to deepen your understanding of what it means to display His glory as a woman.

"TRUE WOMANHOOD IS A DISTINCTIVE CALLING OF GOD TO DISPLAY THE GLORY OF HIS SON IN WAYS THAT WOULD NOT BE DISPLAYED IF THERE WERE NO WOMANHOOD."
— John Piper

incredible story

> *"For the husband is the head of the wife even as Christ is the head of the church, his body, and is himself its Savior."*
>
> **Ephesians 5:23**

> *"The head of a wife is her husband, and the head of Christ is God."*
>
> **I Corinthians 11:3**

> *"We are members of [Christ's] body. 'Therefore a man shall leave his father and mother and hold fast to his wife, and the two shall become one flesh.' This mystery is profound, and I am saying that it refers to Christ and the church."*
>
> **Ephesians 5:30–32**

Yesterday, we learned that male and female were created in the image of God, to reflect the glory of God. We were each designed to be "image-bearers"—to display the likeness of our Creator.

The responsibility to reflect God's image, however, wasn't just given to us as individuals. Mankind was created as male and female—in relationship—to display something about the divine relationship that exists within the triune God. Our relationships were created to tell the incredible story of God.

Describe some ways in which you think a male-female relationship could put God on display.

The bible speaks on a relationship between male & female to be like Christ & the church. To look upon my husband with respect as I follow his leadership

Would you say that most male-female relationships today are doing a good job of displaying the glory of God? Why or why not?

I would say they are not because the role reversals, disrespect, and even lack of love.

We can't fully understand what the image of God is all about, but two things are clear. First, being created in His image gives us enormous dignity, privilege, and responsibility. He has crowned us with honor and glory and given us authority over the earth.

It's a breathtaking charge to go about the business of daily life and all the while reflect the image of the Almighty. And that leads to the second thing: What a mess we've made of this awesome dignity!—especially in male-female relationships.

The image of God in man has been badly marred, sometimes even beyond recognition. It begs for redemption. Transformation. A type of re-creation. And

stunningly enough, before sin ever entered the world, God gave us a picture of His redemptive plan, in the creation of man as male and female.

God knew from the beginning that sin would distort and destroy the male-female relationship. Amazingly, He patterned the first couple's relationship to correspond with the amazing relationship that would one day counter all of the horrible, tragic consequences of sin.

The chart below maps out some corresponding relationships. The arrows represent the headship structure established by God in His Word. Refer to the verses on page 24 to fill in the boxes under the arrows.

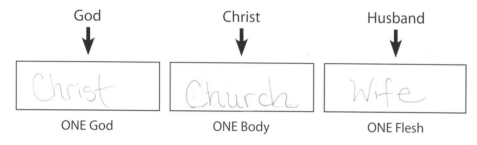

God	Christ	Husband
↓	↓	↓
Christ	Church	Wife
ONE God	ONE Body	ONE Flesh

Did you write "Christ" in the first box? God is the head of Christ. Christ is the head of the church, and the husband is the head of his wife.

There's a clear and corresponding pattern evident in all three relationships. For the moment, don't get distracted thinking about what this all means, how it works out in marriage, or its implication for male-female relationships in general. We'll explore some of those questions later. For now, we just want you to see the pattern and note the biblical parallel between these three relationships.

We want you to grasp that God created male and female and instituted marriage for a specific reason. That reason was revealed and can only be understood in and through Jesus Christ. God created male and female to tell the incredible story of Christ.

Reread Ephesians 5:30–32 in the margin of the previous page. Circle the words "mystery" and "profound." What is the profound mystery?

Marriage

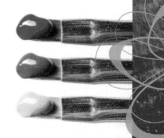

My (Mary's) youngest son, Jonathan, is studying English literature and history at a university in Canada. Jonathan could tell you that good stories often use a literary device called foreshadowing. Foreshadowing is a technique in which an event is hinted at before it happens.

Think back to the last movie you watched. How did the story line forecast the outcome? If it was a good story, it undoubtedly contained subtle hints about how it would end. Even if you were surprised at the ending, you could go back and rewatch the movie and clearly see the hints and clues that pointed toward the ending.

Before time began, before male and female were ever created, God had a splendid plan that He kept a mystery. Throughout the Old Testament, that plan was foreshadowed but hidden from plain view (1 Cor. 2:7; Col. 1:26). It wasn't until Christ died that the mystery of God's eternal purpose—and the ultimate purpose of manhood, womanhood, and marriage—became clear.

Paul connects the dots for us and reveals the stunning beauty of this mystery in the book of Ephesians. In chapter 3 he explains that God's eternal, mysterious plan finally came to light through the work of Jesus Christ (v. 9–10). Then, in chapter 5, he ties the mystery of Christ loving the church to the earthly picture of male-female sexuality and marriage.

According to Scripture, the relationship between a husband and wife is powerfully linked to the story of Christ and His church-bride (see Eph. 5:25–33). God created male and female to foreshadow and testify about THAT amazing relationship and event. That's one of the main reasons why He made us male and female and why He created marriage.

In the opening chapter of his epistle to the Romans, Paul addresses sexual relationships and conduct. In that context, he explains what God wanted to "make plain" through creation—including the apex of His creation, male and female.

"But we impart a secret and hidden wisdom of God, which God decreed before the ages . . ."

1 Corinthians 2:7

"He chose us in him before the foundation of the world... according to the purpose of his will, to the praise of his glorious grace, with which he has blessed us in the Beloved."

Ephesians 1:4–6

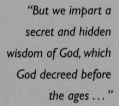

Read Romans 1:19–20 in the margin. What two invisible things did God want to display through His creation?

1. _Eternal Power_

2. _Divine Nature_

God's eternal power and His divine nature find their ultimate expression in Christ. Together, male and female (gender) testify to the character of God and portray the greater reality of Christ and the church. This spiritual truth is so magnificent that God chose to put it on prominent display throughout the entire world. He stamped the trailer for His story on every human being who has ever lived.

Men were created to reflect the strength, love, and self-sacrifice of Christ. Women were created to reflect the responsiveness, grace, and beauty of the bride He redeemed. And marriage was created to reflect the covenant union of Christ and His bride.

Scripture is emphatic that the story line of male and female (and male-female relationships) has little to do with us, and much to do with God. Your womanhood is ultimately not about you. It's about displaying the glory of God and His powerful redemptive plan.

If gender was created to tell the story of God, how important is it that we understand a biblical perspective on womanhood? Put an "X" on the gradient to indicate how important it is:

It's not important   It's extremely important

→ **Can you think of any examples** of how your life and relationships as a woman have—or have not—displayed the image of God and His redemptive story?

rejection, lack of grace, ill behavior

> "FOR WHAT CAN BE KNOWN ABOUT GOD IS PLAIN TO THEM, BECAUSE GOD HAS SHOWN IT TO THEM. FOR HIS INVISIBLE ATTRIBUTES, NAMELY, HIS ETERNAL POWER AND DIVINE NATURE [GODHEAD, NKJV], HAVE BEEN CLEARLY PERCEIVED, EVER SINCE THE CREATION OF THE WORLD, IN THE THINGS THAT HAVE BEEN MADE. SO THEY ARE WITHOUT EXCUSE."
>
> Romans 1:19–20

big picture

*N*icole is a young woman who attended a True Woman conference. She came out of curiosity, and with quite a bit of skepticism. She couldn't understand why it was important to have a conference about womanhood. She hated the thought of the "woman's role" being different than the "man's role"—as if she couldn't do everything a man could do (and better!).

Nicole said her "aha" moment came when she realized that manhood and womanhood exist to display deep, spiritual truths about God.

> When I approached the topic of gender roles from a human perspective, the whole discussion just seemed silly. But then it "clicked" that God wants my womanhood to tell HIS story! And everything started to make sense. I was so wrapped up in thinking my womanhood was about me, my relationships, and what I wanted out of life. I was missing the big picture. Ultimately, my womanhood is not about me. It's about telling the story of Jesus.

Prior to attending the True Woman event, Nicole couldn't see the forest for the trees. "Can't see the forest for the trees!" is an expression used of people who get so wrapped up in the specifics, that they fail to see the big picture. And sadly, this often happens in discussions about manhood and womanhood. People focus on the specifics of gender roles and relationships but lose sight of the greater realities to which they point.

The "can't see the forest for the trees" expression brings to mind the dense conifer forests that cover the slopes of the Rockies and other ranges in the Pacific Northwest. A couple of years ago, we vacationed together in Colorado with a group of friends, and had the thrill of riding an old steam train through a magnificent forest of conifers. The majority of these evergreen forests are populated by two types of trees: ponderosa pine and Douglas fir.

The ponderosa pine has intricately grooved orangey-brown bark, long slender needles, and a faint vanilla smell. The bark of the Douglas fir is dark and deeply furrowed. Its flat, pointy needles spiral around each twig. The smell is distinctively strong and earthy. Each type of tree is beautiful in and of itself. But when viewed together—as a forest surrounded by peaks and

> *"God created man in his own image, in the image of God he created him; male and female he created them."*
>
> **Genesis 1:27**

valleys, sparkling rivers, and a vast expanse of cornflower blue sky—the rich green carpet of trees is absolutely gorgeous!

We hope you caught a glimpse of the "big picture" in yesterday's lesson. It's as though we stood at a high vantage point and took a look at how male and female, like fir and pine, are part of the same forest—and how this one forest fits into the overall landscape of the plans and purposes of God.

Today, we're going to zoom in a bit, so only the forest is in view. We're going to have a look at male and female as members of the human race—and see that both have equal worth, value, and dignity as bearers of God's image. Male and female are equally part of the creation that He called "man."

Read Genesis 1:26–31 in your Bible. In verse 27, who does it say God created in His own image? ☐ man ☐ him ☑ male and female

In an effort to be inclusive (and supposedly less offensive), some modern translations of the Bible have obscured the gender imagery found in the original Hebrew text. They have substituted "human beings" or "humankind" for the word "man," and "them" for the word "him." But in Hebrew, this verse clearly communicates that *"man"* equals *"him"* equals *"male and female."* (Make sure to check all the boxes in the question above.)

You may wonder: Isn't it sexist, discriminatory, and out-of-date to use the generic word "man" for all humans (male and female)? Why does the Bible call humankind "him"? Shouldn't we update the words of the Bible so it doesn't use male pronouns when it speaks of men and women as a group?

How do you feel when the Bible uses male-gendered words like "man" or "brothers" to refer to men and women as a group? Why?

Women came from Man. I think its how a plural usage of the word.

There is an important reason why God uses the word "man" to refer to the human race as a whole. Today's discussion is going to get a bit technical, but please bear with us. Understanding this concept will help you understand the Bible's overall teaching on gender, and also why God often uses male pronouns inclusive of women. Hang in there, and you'll see that this really does matter!

Genesis 1:27 heralds the stunning truth that all humans bear the divine image—men and women bear it equally. But it also states and restates the fact that God refers to us collectively with a singular male pronoun.

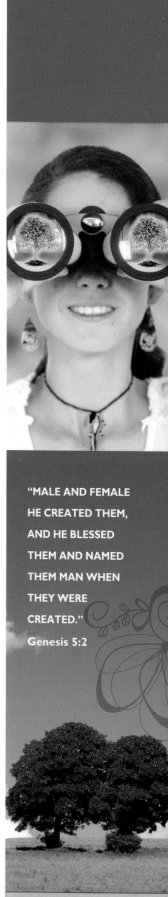

"MALE AND FEMALE HE CREATED THEM, AND HE BLESSED THEM AND NAMED THEM MAN WHEN THEY WERE CREATED."
Genesis 5:2

In Genesis 5:2 in the margin, circle the phrase "named them Man." Why do you think God chose this common name for male and female?

_____

_____

We've been taught that using the word "man" to refer to the human race demeans women. But a closer look reveals that the exact opposite is true. In choosing the word "man" as the common name for male and female, God indicated that male and female would share a common condition for which He would provide a common solution.

When God called male and female "man," He actually underlined the profound unity and equality that exist between us. This common name shows that woman comes from man and is not independent of him. It shows that both sexes exist to tell the story of God, and that this story is told together—with male and female as parts of a unified whole. The common name "man" demonstrates that in the end, the story line of gender isn't about male _or_ female—it's not about us at all—it's about _the_ Man, Jesus Christ, whose redemptive work applies to both sexes equally.

You see, the Hebrew word for "man" is _'adam_. It's closely related to the word for ground, _adamah_. It's a generic term that refers to all human beings, whether male or female. After the fall, "Adam" (capital "A") becomes the proper name of the first male. And much later, Jesus Christ comes as "the last Adam" to redeem _'adam_ (mankind) and bring many sons and daughters of God to glory. The connection between these words can be illustrated like this:

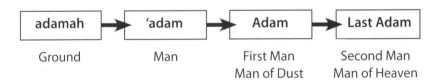

adamah	'adam	Adam	Last Adam
Ground	Man	First Man Man of Dust	Second Man Man of Heaven

Circle the part of the chart above that refers to Jesus Christ. Put a box around the part that refers to male and female.

In God's eyes, the female is as much a part and expression of _'adam_ as the male. If you take a moment to think about it, the implications are staggering. This means that both male and female can trace their beginnings to the dirt of the ground. It means that both bear God's image fully and individually. It means that God values both equally.

"Male and female he created them, and he blessed them and named them Man when they were created."

Genesis 5:2

"The first man Adam became a living being; the last Adam became a life-giving spirit."

I Corinthians 15:45

"For as in Adam all die, so also in Christ shall all be made alive."

I Corinthians 15:22

Because both are *'adam*, both are equally represented by the first man, Adam. Both are fallen and in need of a Savior. The good news of the gospel is that both are also equally represented by the second Man—the last Adam— Jesus Christ. Together, redeemed men and women make up the church He loves, the bride He sacrificed His life to redeem. Male and female are indivisibly connected. Together—united as a whole—they tell the story of the gospel.

Using the analogy of the conifer forest, we can say that although man and woman—like pine and fir—are different, we are equally part of the forest, equally evergreen, and equally important to the forest's ecosystem.

When God named male and female *'adam*, He had the last Adam in mind. So when, in order to appease modern sensibilities, we change "man" to something we think is more "inclusive," we diminish the true meaning of the word. If woman is not part of "man," then how can she be represented by the first man, Adam? What's more, how can she be represented by the second Man, the last Adam, Jesus Christ?

That may all be a bit difficult to grasp, but here's the point we want you to get: It is foolish to think that we can improve on the Bible's teaching on gender or the gender language it uses. The big picture informs us that from the very beginning, God's plan for gender has little to do with us and everything to do with Jesus. And we need to trust that even if we don't fully understand them, the words, images, and means He has chosen to display His glory are not only right, they are also good. Very good!

In your Bible, read 1 Corinthians 15:45–49. Summarize why God groups males and females together and calls them "man."

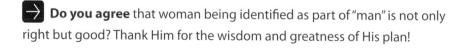

→ **Do you agree** that woman being identified as part of "man" is not only right but good? Thank Him for the wisdom and greatness of His plan!

cosmic significance

*W*e hope you're starting to see that God had an important, specific reason in mind for creating male and female, and that the reason had little to do with men or women, and much to do with God. He created the sexes to put important truths about the gospel on display. He wanted male and female to tell the same story in different ways.

Males display the glory of God in a uniquely masculine way. Females display the glory of God in a uniquely feminine way. Each sex bears the image of God; but together, they display deep, important truths about God in relationship—God the Father in relationship with the Son of God, and the Son of God in relationship with His bride.

Remember the pine and fir? Each is green, and a conifer in its own right. But the presence of two types of trees brings greater depth of color and texture to the forest. A forest with a mix of pine and fir has a different look to it than one with only pine or only fir. When both are present, the splendor of the whole forest is enhanced.

Wouldn't it be silly for the ponderosa pine and the Douglas fir to get into a debate about which type of tree is more vital to the forest? Wouldn't it be

foolish for the ponderosa to insist that the fir ought to give off a pleasant vanilla smell instead of a strong, earthy one? Or for the fir to argue that its flat, pointy needles are better than the long, slender needles of the ponderosa?

A debate like this would be absolutely ridiculous! It's obvious that though the trees are different, they are both beautiful. Both are significant to the forest's ecosystem. They are different AND equal. Neither is better than the other. It would be absurd for them to play the comparison game, criticize each other, and put each other down on account of their differences. But sadly, this is what often happens between male and female.

When God stamped His image on us, He crowned us with unsurpassed dignity and worth. Because of this, men and women ought to treat each other with deep respect. As theologian Wayne Grudem says,

Every time we look at each other or talk to each other as men and women, we should remember that the person we are talking to is a creature of God who is more like God than anything else in the universe, and men and women share that status equally.[1]

Sadly, however, since sin entered the picture, men and women do not always treat each other with the respect that ought to flow out of our equal standing as image-bearers of God.

It breaks our hearts when we see men treating women, or women treating men, as inferior beings. It also breaks God's heart. One-upmanship, manipulation, words that belittle or demean, abusive behavior—these are an attack on the very image of God. The book of James addresses the issue of "[cursing] people who are made in the likeness of God" and concludes: "these things ought not to be so" (James 3:9–10)!

profound significance and worth

The first chapter of Genesis contains twelve indicators that confirm the profound significance and the equal worth of male and female. They remind us that God does not favor or value one sex over the other. He loves and values men and women equally.

Read Genesis 1:26–31 in your Bible, and note the twelve "equality indicators" below:

Twelve Equality Indicators

1. Both are created for God's **glory** (1:26; Isa. 43:7).
2. Both are **named** *'adam* (1:26–27; Gen. 5:2).
3. Both are **created** by the hand of God (1:27).
4. Both are created in the **image** of God (1:26–27).
5. Both are made after God's **likeness** (1:26).
6. Both are **blessed** by God (1:28).
7. Both are charged to be **fruitful** and multiply (1:28).
8. Both are given **dominion** over the earth (1:26, 28).
9. Both are recipients of God's **provision** (1:29).
10. Both have a personal **relationship** with God (1:28; Gen. 3:8–13).
11. Both are **accountable** to God (1:28; Gen. 3:11–13).
12. Both are **heirs** of the grace of life (1:27; Gen. 3:15; 1 Peter 3:7).

Based on the equality indicators in Genesis, do you think the Lord would approve of one sex claiming superiority or putting the other down? Why or why not?

_____

_____

Have you ever been guilty of putting someone down because of their sex— or of treating them with less than the respect they deserve as a creation of God and a bearer of His image?

_____

_____

Created in the image of the infinite God, the significance of both man and woman is beyond measure.

We hope you don't just agree to this truth intellectually but that you also feel it personally and deeply. It's a mind-blowing wonder that the Maker stamped His image equally on every human being who has ever lived—including you! That attaches profound significance to your life!

Read Psalm 8:4–6 in the margin. How do you feel about the fact that you have been created in the image of God—that He is "mindful" of you and has crowned you with glory and honor?

_____

_____

So many women struggle with their sense of worth. The world tries to convince us that we need to enhance our sense of self-worth. It encourages women to draw their worth from looks, education, careers, possessions, relationships, and their individual personalities and abilities.

The Bible's view on worth is much different than that of popular culture. It teaches that we don't need a greater sense of "*self*-worth" . . . what we desperately need is a greater sense of "*His*-worth."

When we see God as He is—in His awesome greatness, majesty, goodness, and love—we will have a proper perspective on ourselves. We will marvel at what it means to be created in His likeness and to be loved by Him. And we will be motivated to treat others with respect and grace, recognizing that even the most depraved sinner is a bearer of His image, distorted as that image may be.

What are some of the places you look to find your sense of value and worth?

_____

_____

Explain how you think your life would change if you were to more fully grasp the truth that God created you in His image—to display His glory—and that THAT is what gives you worth and significance?

_____

_____

How could the truth that every person is created in the image of God change your attitude or behavior toward a difficult person in your life?

_____

_____

"yes, Lord!"

*B*etween the two of us, we've been to scores of women's events over the years. At many of these, attendees received canvas tote bags of free stuff like books, hand cream, Kleenex, trinkets, chocolates, promo items . . . (you know the routine —gotta love those tote bags!). We figure we've seen just about all there is to see when it comes to the contents of these bags. But the tote bags at True Woman conferences include an item we've never received at another conference: a white cloth handkerchief.

Now I (Mary) am not much for women's hankies. I remember receiving several lacy embroidered ones from my grandmother, who thought I'd appreciate their dainty feminine look. But I was a tomboy. I hated them. They did come in handy when I needed to polish my rock collection. In my mind, that's the only thing they were good for.

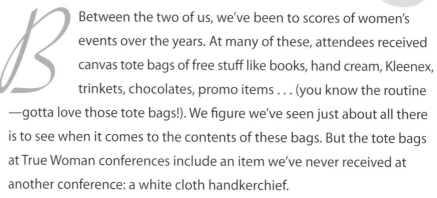

My five brothers would have mocked me relentlessly had I ever pulled a lace hankie from my jeans. So, as you can well imagine, I wasn't initially impressed by this tote-bag treasure. Though it wasn't lacy, it was white . . . and was embroidered with the True Woman logo and the motto "Yes, Lord!"

At the first True Woman conference, when Nancy encouraged us to wave our white hankies in the air before the Lord as a symbol of surrender, I must confess that "Hooray!" wasn't the first thought that came to mind. Quite honestly, the idea sounded a bit silly. But then I began to ponder why I emotionally resisted this simple symbolic act.

I concluded that it's one thing to say "Yes, Lord" with my mouth—and quite another thing to say "Yes, Lord" with my actions. Participating in such a visible symbol was just so . . . visible. Others would see. And therein lay the rub. Was I willing to stand and say "Yes, Lord" when doing so was uncomfortable or challenged my pride? Was I, like David, willing to "become even more undignified than this" in worship of the God I love (2 Sam. 6:22 NIV)?

The hankie embroidered with the words "Yes, Lord" symbolizes the central message of the True Woman movement. Being a True Woman means saying yes to Jesus—and yes to the things God says about womanhood and the way we ought to live our lives. And that means saying no to the other voices that clamor for our attention—those voices on TV, the Internet, magazines, ads, and a thousand other places that tell us what women should be—how we should think, dress, and act, what we should aspire to, and how to conduct ourselves in our relationships with men.

Having a heart and life that say "Yes, Lord!" is a hallmark of what it means to be a Christian. Jesus said that those who love Him would keep His commandments (John 14:15). Obedience is an evidence that we are truly children of God (1 Peter 1:14; see also Heb. 5:9; 11:8). In fact, according to Scripture, those who persistently disobey His Word, those who have no inclination to obey Him, have no basis for assurance that they belong to Him.

Read 1 John 2:3–5 in your Bible. What are the implications of this passage as we consider what God's Word has to say about womanhood?

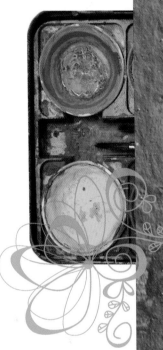

_____

_____

Put a mark on the scale to indicate how you feel about saying yes to what the Bible says about womanhood:

I feel unsure or   I feel eager
reluctant   and willing

Explain why you feel this way:

_____

_____

If you say yes to the Lord, you will often find yourself swimming upstream against popular culture—and in many cases, even against the culture of womanhood prevalent among Christians.

But discovering and embracing God's design for your life will bring incredible blessing and joy. You will discover your true identity and purpose. You will become more "you"—more of whom He created you to be. In addition, your relationships

will grow and be strengthened, and your life will point others to Christ and encourage them to say "Yes, Lord" as well.

That was the experience of a group of over a hundred women who flew all the way from the Dominican Republic to attend the first True Woman conference in Chicago. These women were unusually hungry-hearted—eager to receive and respond to God's truth. Along with thousands of other participants, they waved their white hankies throughout the conference, as a symbolic way of saying "Yes, Lord!"

They returned home committed to live out the implications of that surrender. They began seeking His "divine design" in relation to every area of their lives—their values, priorities, relationships, families, careers—everything! Many experienced newfound gratitude for their calling as women; they embraced the challenge to pass the baton of truth on to the next generation (one woman expressed that she had always thought mentoring younger women was for *other* women, not for her!).

For many of those women, saying "Yes, Lord" required adjustments that proved to be countercultural and costly. One woman, for example, felt led to make drastic cuts in her hours at her successful dental practice, so she could more effectively meet the needs of her husband and children. Two women, upon learning that their husbands had been unfaithful in the past, found grace to truly forgive for Christ's sake, and to restore their marriages.

Over the next few months, the transformation in the lives of these Dominican women had a profound effect, as many of their husbands, along with others in their churches, began to take the Lord more seriously and to deal with issues in their own lives. To this day, the Spirit is moving in a significant way in and through the lives of those women.

What kind of impact do you think might be made if multitudes of Christian women were to say "Yes, Lord!" to His biblical design for their lives as women?

To see a video clip showing the impact of the True Woman movement in the Dominican Republic, go to www.TrueWoman.com/ DominicanRepublic.

womanhood matters

We're so glad you've decided to join us on this journey of discovering what True Womanhood is about. You may be eager to discover more about this divine design. But you may be among those who are not so sure how they feel about this thing called "biblical womanhood." It may help you to know that there was a time when we both felt the same way.

I (Nancy) will confess that I have not always been enthused about the fact that God made me a woman. As a younger woman who earnestly wanted to

serve the Lord and have a life that "counts," I had an underlying, unvoiced feeling that if I had been a man, I could have been more useful to His kingdom. I lacked a clear vision of God's distinctive mission and calling for women.

However, in my late twenties and early thirties, as I began to discover what His Word has to say about why He created male and female, what the distinctions mean and why they matter, and how He wants to use both men and women in His redemptive plan, I began to develop a sense of genuine joy and gratitude for the privilege of being a woman.

I (Mary) can echo some of Nancy's sentiments. We both grew up as the women's movement was really taking off and long-held traditional views of

womanhood were being challenged. I'm the only girl in a family with five boys—the only one of all my siblings who got a university degree and embarked on a professional career. The Lord has given me many capabilities. What's more, I have a strong, independent personality. The pull for me to embrace the world's ideas about womanhood has been intense at times.

Discovering God's divine design for womanhood, and figuring out how to live that out as a wife and mom (Mary) and a single woman (Nancy), has been an ongoing journey. It will be a journey for you too. But we can assure you it will be worth every bit of the time and effort!

We hope you've discovered, in this first week, why womanhood is important, and why it's vital that you explore and wrestle with the meaning and implications of True Womanhood from God's perspective.

In the space below, summarize what you've learned this week about God's plan for womanhood, and why womanhood is important:

_____

_____

→ **Conclude this week's lessons** by writing out a prayer, asking Him to teach you more about what womanhood means, and to help you grow to be a True Woman of God.

drawing it out, drawing it in . . .

gender matters

process

The video for Week One will help you process this week's lessons. You'll find this week's video, a downloadable outline/listening guide, and many more resources at www.TrueWoman101.com/week1.

ponder:

Think about the following questions. Discuss them with your friends, family, and/or small group:

1. Does gender matter, or are we free to define it as we wish?

2. What does Scripture's account of creation indicate about God's design for male and female? (See Gen. 1:26–2:25.)

3. What did God hope to accomplish with His design for gender?

4. How is it possible that the two sexes are different yet equal?

5. What are some ways in which a male-female relationship might put God on display?

6. How important is it that women understand God's design for womanhood? Why?

7. Do you feel that God's design for manhood and womanhood is "very good"? Explain.

8. Have you wholeheartedly said yes to God's design? Is there any part of your heart that feels reluctant or is holding back?

personalize:

Use the following lined page to journal. Write down what you learned this week. Record your comments, a favorite verse, or a concept or quote that was particularly helpful or meaningful to you. Compose a prayer, letter, or poem. Jot down notes from the video or your small group session. Express your heart response to what you have studied. Personalize this week's lessons in the way that will best help you apply them to your life.

personalize it

drawing it out,
drawing it in . . .

snips & snails

There's an old Mother Goose nursery rhyme, dating back to the early nineteenth century that talks about the difference between boys and girls:

What are little boys made of?

"Snips and snails, and puppy dogs' tails
That's what little boys are made of!"

What are little girls made of?

"Sugar and spice and all things nice
That's what little girls are made of!"

The poem was written in an era that assigned gentle traits to girls and rough-and-tumble behaviors to boys—an era that had clear ideas about the differing strengths, roles, and responsibilities of men and women.

Dissatisfied with these kinds of stereotypes, the feminist movement sought to redefine womanhood. It worked to minimize distinctions and overcome role differences between the sexes. It promoted the idea that women were powerful, strong, and invincible. Women didn't need men; they didn't want to be stifled by traditional definitions of womanhood—especially not by the roles of "wife" and "mom."

Feminists suggested that men didn't possess any qualities that were different or unique. In fact, when compared to the female, the male was actually inferior: "Everything guys can do, girls can do better!" They claimed that women would not be equal to men until they filled the same roles and positions as men. Equality, they insisted, means role interchangeability. If male and female roles are different, then they aren't really equal.

Modern culture has accepted the feminist idea that differences between male and female are inconsequential to the roles we assume. In contrast to the Mother Goose era, we now view roles as *interchangeable*—it doesn't matter who wears the pants. A mom can be as good a dad as a dad; a dad can be as good a mom as a mom. We also view male-female roles as *malleable*— we get to shape and define what the roles are. Culture wants us to think that all definitions of gender, sexual relationships, marriage, motherhood, fatherhood, and family are equally valid.

Many people today view male-female distinctions as utterly irrelevant and *dispensable*. As newly married and first-time mother, reality TV star Bethenny Frankel told *People* magazine in an "Up Close" video interview, "Jason's an incredible father. He is nurturing. He changes 95% of the diapers. There is no woman/man in this relationship—except for the fact [crudeness alert] that I have the boobs and the baby came out of me!"[1]

In the modern feminist worldview, we get to decide what girls are made of. We can decide for ourselves what our womanhood means and what role we want to assume. So much for Mother Goose. If we want, we can drop the *sugar*, and add some *snips and snails* to our *spice*.

Though the formula of snips, snails, and tails for boys and sugar and spice for girls can be shrugged off as childish, the questions posed by this nursery rhyme are valid. What are little boys made of? What are little girls made of? Is there a difference? And if there is, what implication does that have for our lives?

This week we're going to address the first question: "What are little boys made of?" We're going to take a close look at Genesis and examine God's creation of man. We'll learn about how God wired men, and what makes them tick. Next week, and for much of the rest of the study, we're going to focus on women. But in order to grasp what God had in mind for us girls, it's important that we first understand what He had in mind for the guys. Boys aren't made of snips and snails and puppy dog tails; but as you'll soon see, they *were* created with a unique purpose and design. →

boys will be boys

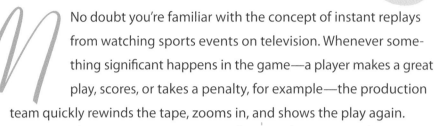

*N*o doubt you're familiar with the concept of instant replays from watching sports events on television. Whenever something significant happens in the game—a player makes a great play, scores, or takes a penalty, for example—the production team quickly rewinds the tape, zooms in, and shows the play again.

I (Mary) have come to appreciate and expect the instant replay—especially since my son, Matt, moved away from home to play professional hockey. I can't be at many of his games in person, but I can watch on TV or the Internet. When Matt does something noteworthy, I know they'll show the play again. So I lean in to the screen and pay close attention.

Seeing the play again close-up, and perhaps from a different angle, gives me a better view of what really happened. I see things I didn't see the first time around. The replay helps me analyze all the details. I get to see how the play unfolded, Matt's part in it, and maybe even the expression on his face.

The first "instant replay" is recorded in Genesis, long before the days of big-screen TV (or hockey). Genesis 1 gives an overview of what took place in the seven days of creation. In chapter 2, it's as though the producer rewinds the tape, zooms in, and replays the game-winning play of creation from a different angle and in slow motion, so viewers can see every detail.

Why do you think Scripture "rewinds the tape" and "zooms in" to show a detailed replay of the creation of male and female?

_____

_____

up close and personal

In the first chapter, we learned that the story line of gender is ultimately about displaying the glory of our Creator. It's an object lesson—a sort of parable—that teaches us about the relationship between Christ and His bride.

The truth that God wanted to display His glory through male and female was of paramount importance. So it stands to reason that He was highly

---

"Then the LORD God formed the man of dust from the ground and breathed into his nostrils the breath of life, and the man became a living creature. And the LORD God planted a garden in Eden, in the east, and there he put the man whom he had formed."

Genesis 2:7–8

"But now, O LORD, you are our Father; we are the clay, and you are our potter; we are all the work of your hand."

Isaiah 64:8

intentional when He created them. Every detail was significant. That's why Genesis chapter 2 zooms in and provides a slow-motion replay.

In Genesis 1, we see that the Lord spoke creation into existence by the power of His Word. But in the zoomed-in view of Genesis 2, we see that He got up close and personal when He created the sexes.

Read Genesis 2:4–8 in your Bible. In the verses in the margin, circle the phrase "the Lord God formed the man of dust from the ground." Describe (or draw) the image that comes to mind when you think of Him "forming" man.

_____

_____

What are the implications of this passage? Read the following statements and mark whether you think each implication is true [T] or false [F].

_____ God was intentional about the way He made man.
_____ God shaped man like a potter shapes a piece of clay.
_____ God let the man determine his own design and purpose.
_____ God created man with a unique connection to "the ground."
_____ Man's spirit came directly from the breath of God.

Can you think of any other implications?

_____

_____

The Hebrew word for "formed" is the same word that is used of a potter forming and shaping clay. It suggests an artistic, inventive activity that requires skill and planning—a work that is done with great care and precision.

Have you ever seen a potter at work? It's fascinating to watch the process of an unattractive lump of clay being spun around, then carefully molded and shaped by the potter's hands until it becomes the work of art he originally envisioned and designed.

We can only faintly imagine what it must have been like for God to take simple, inanimate dust from the ground and to skillfully, thoughtfully fashion it into a man with countless atoms, cells, organs, and complex, intricate systems that mystify the most brilliant scientists! And then, wonder of wonders—for God to breathe His own breath into the form so that the man became a living soul, a reflection of His own likeness!

More amazing yet, God didn't just take a personal interest in the creation of Adam—He oversees the creation of *every* human being, each one with his or her distinctive appearance, DNA, personality, natural abilities, etc.

Read Psalm 139:14–16 in the margin, where David reflects on his own creation. What do these verses imply about God's role in the creation of every detail of our lives, including our gender?

"I praise you, for I am fearfully and wonderfully made. Wonderful are your works; my soul knows it very well. My frame was not hidden from you, when I was being made in secret, intricately woven in the depths of the earth. Your eyes saw my unformed substance; in your book were written, every one of them, the days that were formed for me, when as yet there was none of them."

Psalm 139:14–16

God did not create the sexes haphazardly. When He created the male, He wove him together intricately, according to the design He had in mind. Before the creation of the world, He saw man's unformed substance. Before a star or tree or fish was created, man's existence was written in God's "book" (Ps. 139:16; cf. Eph. 1:4–5).

When as yet there were no male and no female, God had a plan. He wrote the story. He knew the ending. And He carefully crafted male and female to put the glory of this spectacular story on display.

No wonder God got up close and personal when He created male and female! You can be sure that nothing about the sexes was created arbitrarily or by chance. Let's go back to Genesis 2 and observe some details about Adam's creation that give us important insight into God's design for men.

Read Genesis 2:7–8. Was Adam created inside or outside of the garden? Why do you think God created him there?

What did God do *after* He created Adam (v. 8)?

_____

_____

God created man out of the dust of the ground. Then He placed him in a garden in the land of Eden. The Hebrew word for "garden" indicates an enclosure, a plot of ground protected by a wall or hedge. It's an area with specified boundaries—a place shielded from danger. The garden plot was in the land of "Eden," a word that many scholars believe means "delight." This designated space was to be the man's new home, where he would be joined with a wife and start a family. All of these details are significant.

Later in Genesis 2 we see that when a man gets married, he leaves his family of origin, in order to initiate a new family unit ("*a man shall leave* his father and his mother and hold fast to his wife"—v. 24). So when God put His firstborn male in the garden, it appears that He had this pattern in mind. God set the man up in his own place to be the head of a new home.

The man's responsibility to "leave," "hold fast," and launch a new family unit indicates that *taking initiative is at the core of what it means to be a man*. God doesn't want boys to remain boys. He wants them to become men! He wants them to grow up, "leave" their moms and dads, launch out, start new households, and become the men He created them to be.

Do you think our culture generally encourages men to grow up and take initiative, as God designed? Can you think of any examples to support your answer?

_____

_____

In what way does the responsibility of man to take initiative mirror what Jesus does for the church?

_____

_____

men at work

Every time Atlanta's Cynthia Good drove by a "Men at Work" sign, it irked her. The founding editor of the professional woman's magazine *PINK*, Ms. Good considered the signs to be a subtle form of discrimination. After all, it's not just men who work—women work too!

One day, the police showed up on Good's doorstep to investigate a complaint that she had defaced a sign by spray-painting a large, bright "WO" in front of the word "Men Working." While she didn't admit to the graffiti, she proceeded to lodge complaints about the sexist signs to the public works commissioner, the mayor of Atlanta, and the governor of Georgia.

In response to her complaint, and notwithstanding the cost, Atlanta painted over the city signs to read "Workers" or "Workers Ahead." What's more, state officials subsequently demanded that private contractors remove all signs that imply that it's just men doing the work.

Not content to let the campaign for gender neutrality stop in Atlanta, the crusading editor took her cause nationwide. Because of Cynthia Good, "Men at Work" signs have now become as extinct as the dodo.

Today, many folks would find "Men at Work" signs objectionable. Many would also find the Bible objectionable—because right from the get-go, it posts all sorts of "signs" about men working. God gave men a responsibility to work that is unique to what it means to be a man. Work is foundational to manhood in a way that it isn't foundational to womanhood.

Don't get me wrong. That's not to say that women don't work, or can't work, or don't want to work, or should never work outside of the home. That's nonsense, and not at all what the Bible teaches. Right up front, let's be clear about that! However, it *does* mean that male and female are different. As part of our God-created "wiring," man is connected to "work" in a way woman is not; and woman is connected to home and relationships in a way man is not. Obviously, that doesn't mean that a woman is incapable of working, or that a man is incapable of creating a home and relating, or that they do not ever do these things. It just means that God created male

and female with differing natural "bents" and spheres of responsibility. The male was created with a unique responsibility to work to provide for the family, and the female was created with a unique responsibility to nest and to nurture family relationships.

We'll talk more about woman's role later. But for now, let's turn back to Genesis to see how God created man with a unique responsibility to be a provider.

In your Bible, read the verses listed below. Draw lines matching the reference in the left column to its matching summary statement on the right.

Genesis 2:5–7	Sin made man's *work* much more difficult.
Genesis 2:15	God sent the man out of the garden to *work* the field.
Genesis 3:17–19	God created man from the dust of the ground he would one day *work*.
Genesis 3:23	God assigned the man to *work* the garden.

Why do you think that God specifically associated man (and not woman) with "work"?

_____

_____

How do you feel about the fact that the Bible makes this sex-specific association?

_____

_____

_____

_____

it's off to work we go

The Bible word translated "work" (Hebrew *abad*) is the common word for tilling soil or for other labor (e.g., Isa. 19:9). It implies serving someone other than oneself (Gen. 29:15). It also frequently describes the duties of priests in worship.

The "work" that God assigned to man wasn't about the man earning money to selfishly spend on the latest gadget, toy, or video game. It wasn't about the man gaining power. It wasn't about him gaining prestige. It wasn't so the man could self-actualize. No. God wanted man to work selflessly on behalf of his family. He commissioned the man to use his strength to serve *their* needs, a role Scripture affirms in passages such as 1 Timothy 5:8. Being a "provider"—physically, spiritually, and in other ways—is foundational to manhood. *Working to provide for others (especially those in his family) is at the core of what it means to be a man.*

Does the last sentence resonate with you? Have you noticed that men generally have a greater natural "bent" to be providers? In the space below, write down the names of one or more male friends or family members who exemplify this trait.

In what way does the responsibility of man to selflessly provide for others mirror what Jesus does for the church?

Researchers report that men suffer greater levels of depression and stress during periods of unemployment than women do. Some argue that men just need to "get over it," stop being hung up on traditional roles, and learn to be content being home looking after kids. But Genesis indicates that it's not quite so simple. Gender roles aren't arbitrary. They touch on the core of who God created us to be. According to His design, the concept of "Men Working" is a proper and positive thing!

provide & protect

Read Genesis 2:15 in the margin. Complete the sentence below, filling in the two verbs (action words) that indicate what God expected the male to do for his new "home":

God commanded the man to _____ the garden and
_____ it.

Look up the word "keep" in a thesaurus. (You can find one online at www.thesaurus.com.) In the space below, list the words you think relate most closely to what God expected the man to do:

_____

_____

Besides work, God wanted the man to "keep" the garden. *Keep* translates a Hebrew verb meaning "to be in charge of." It means to guard, protect, and look after. It involves attending to and protecting the persons (Gen. 4:9; 28:15) and property (Gen. 30:31) under one's charge. "Keeping" extends beyond the physical to include a spiritual component of protection (Num. 3:7–8; Ps. 121:3–8).

God created man to be a protector. He gave him the capacity and the inclination to defend. He's the guy who'll fight the enemy, take the bullet, and protect those under his care. It's his responsibility to look out for their well-being and keep them safe. *Being a protector is at the core of what it means to be a man.*

Can you think of an instance in which a male family member or friend exemplified this trait?

_____

_____

In what way does the responsibility of man to defend and protect mirror what Jesus does for the church?

_____

_____

"THE LORD GOD TOOK THE MAN AND PUT HIM IN THE GARDEN OF EDEN TO WORK IT AND KEEP IT."
Genesis 2:15

wearing the pants

Before God created a wife for Adam, it appears the Lord wanted to teach him some of the responsibilities involved in being a man.

In yesterday's lesson, we saw that God put the man in a "home" (the garden of Eden), and gave him the responsibility to provide and protect. We also talked about the fact that this is a reflection of what Christ does for His bride.

Read Ephesians 5:28–29 in the margin. Fill in the blanks with the two verbs (action words) that indicate what Christ does for the church.

1. _____

2. _____

"In the same way husbands should love their wives as their own bodies. He who loves his wife loves himself. For no one ever hated his own flesh, but nourishes and cherishes it, just as Christ does the church."

Ephesians 5:28–29

According to Ephesians 5, the Lord wants men to nourish and cherish their wives just as Christ does the church. To *nourish* is to feed and make grow. It suggests *providing* what is necessary for another person to "bloom" and flourish. Nourish indicates that the provision man is to supply is far more than just physical. "Bringing home the bacon" isn't enough. He's also supposed to support, sustain, and supply the spiritual needs of those under his care.

To *cherish* is to keep or guard carefully, to hold dear, to treat with kindness and care. To cherish someone is to take personal interest in them and to be concerned for their *protection*. The Greek word literally means "to make warm." God created the man to protect and keep the woman "warm"—to keep her safe from harm, physically and spiritually.

The New Testament directive for a man to *nourish* and *cherish* his wife closely corresponds to the responsibility God originally gave man in the garden. *Nourish* relates to man's responsibility to provide, while *cherish* relates to his responsibility to protect.

What do you think it means for a man to provide for (nourish) his wife?

_____

_____

What do you think it means for a man to protect (cherish) his wife?

_____

_____

Man is accountable to God to nourish (provide) and cherish (protect) those in his sphere of responsibility. His primary responsibility is toward his wife. But the charge also extends, in a general way, to the attitude men ought to have toward all women. It is part and parcel of their distinctive, God-created makeup. *Being a protector and provider is at the core of what it means to be a man.*

Can you think of an example of how a man might appropriately provide for or protect a woman who is not his wife?

_____

_____

As a single woman, I (Nancy) am especially grateful for men who are "gentle-men"—for men who have kindly helped me heft a suitcase into an overhead bin on a plane; for the man who made sure my doors were locked at night when he and his wife stayed in my home recently; for a financial advisor who, at his wife's encouragement, has offered to help me with some financial questions; for men who, along with their wives, take time to pray with me or provide counsel or assistance on practical matters.

Sadly, many men are not so considerate and selfless (as is also true of many women). This is a source of discouragement and pain to many women. But it really should come as no surprise. Genesis presents God's original design before sin entered the world and messed everything up. God's ideal for men (and women) will never be perfectly attained in a fallen world. Yet, through Christ's work on the cross, both men and women can be redeemed and find grace to live out their divine design.

How do feel about the fact that God requires men to step up to the plate as providers and protectors?

_____

_____

feed and lead

Genesis indicates that there's a unique spiritual responsibility and also an element of authority associated with what it means to be male. God knew ahead of time that He would create woman as a perfect counterpart to man. But before He created her, He took the time to mentor the man and give him some personal spiritual instruction.

Read Genesis 2:16–17 in the margin. To whom did God communicate the dos and don'ts for the garden? How do you think Eve was expected to learn God's instructions?

_____

_____

What do you think God's actions imply about a man's responsibility?

_____

_____

God communicated His instruction directly to the man. It appears that it was up to the man to pass on God's spiritual instruction to his wife. That's not to suggest that she didn't have her own relationship with the Lord. But it does indicate that as leader of his household, the man had a unique responsibility to learn and understand the ways of the Lord. This was so he could fulfill his commission to provide spiritual oversight and protection. _Exercising spiritual oversight is at the core of what it means to be a man._

Please don't misunderstand. The fact that the male has a unique spiritual responsibility does not absolve the female of spiritual responsibility. When Satan tempted Eve, God held her responsible for knowing and obeying His directives. But God expects men to shoulder spiritual responsibility for their families in a way that is different than the way woman shoulders it.

Read Genesis 2:18–20. Summarize what happened after God gave instructions to the man.

God knew He was going to create woman. Our Creator wasn't frantically searching to find a suitable counterpart for man amongst the animals, wringing His hands in hopes that one of them would do. No. Women were also written into His plan before the foundation of the earth. God knew He would create woman out of a rib that He would extract from the man's side.

So why did God make the man participate in this extensive "name-that-animal" exercise? The task might have gone more quickly with the woman around to help. What possible purpose could He have had in mind?

What purpose do you think the "name-that-animal" exercise might have served in Adam's life?

Adam's naming the animals appears to be a type of training exercise. To name something is to exercise authority over it (cf. Gen. 5:2; Dan. 1:7). The Lord wanted the male to learn how to exercise authority in a godly manner. He wanted the man to learn to attend to someone other than himself, to learn how to serve, and to learn to exercise authority with gentleness, kindness, wisdom, and much care. *Exercising godly leadership is at the core of what it means to be a man.*

That doesn't mean that woman has no authority or leadership responsibility. Genesis 1 indicates that God gave "dominion over the earth" to men and women together. But the fact that God specifically gave the man the responsibility to name the animals indicates that He has given unique and distinct authority to men that is not interchangeable with that of women.

What does God's design for men reveal about His heart toward women?

man of the house

"But for Adam there was not found a helper fit for him. So the LORD God caused a deep sleep to fall upon the man, and while he slept took one of his ribs and closed up its place with flesh. And the rib that the LORD God had taken from the man he made into a woman."

Genesis 2:20–22

"For man was not made from woman, but woman from man....That is why a wife ought to have a symbol of authority on her head."

1 Corinthians 11:8–10

Remember Adam's "name-that-animal" task? Yesterday we learned that God put the man through the paces of this training exercise before He created woman. It seems God wanted to mentor the male in how to exercise authority in a godly manner. The man needed to learn that "wearing the pants" meant selfless, loving service. He needed to learn how to be a man before he was ready to relate to a woman. But we think the training process also served another purpose.

The lengthy process of naming the animals undoubtedly made Adam aware of his deep heart longing. It awakened him to his lack of a suitable mate. Perhaps the Lord wanted the man to catch a glimpse of the full import of God's final and most magnificent work before He drew the woman from Adam's side. Perhaps He wanted the man to feel the longing intensely—to love and want a soul mate with the same sort of passion that Christ felt for His future bride.

> *[Christ] fulfilled what had been signified in Adam: for when Adam was asleep, a rib was drawn from him and Eve was created; so also while the Lord slept on the Cross, His side was transfixed with a spear . . . whence the Church was born. For the Church the Lord's Bride was created from His side, as Eve was created from the side of Adam.*
>
> **— Augustine**

Read Genesis 2:20–22 in the margin and the quote above. What imagery did Augustine see in the creation of the woman from the side of man?

_____

_____

Knowing that God created man and woman to display the cosmic love story of Christ and the church helps us understand our divine design. As we've pointed out previously, who we are as male and female has little to

do with us, and much to do with God. Ultimately, the reason gender roles exist is to make God more knowable. The covenant union between a man and wife provides a tangible picture of what a relationship with God is all about.

God could have made male and female at the exact same time and in the exact same way. He could have given us identical roles. But He didn't. He created the man first. And He gave the male a unique charge to protect, feed, and lead. You may think that the fact the male was created first is trivial or inconsequential, but Scripture teaches otherwise.

Read 1 Corinthians 11:8–10 in the margin of the previous page. (You may want to read verses 2–12 in your Bible, to get the fuller context.) What reason does Scripture give for a wife being under the authority of her husband?

_____

_____

Does this reason make sense to you? Why do you think Scripture teaches that being created first places the man in a position of authority?

_____

_____

As the firstborn of seven children, I (Nancy) feel a special sense of responsibility to provide a godly example and to exercise wise influence in my family.

In the Scripture, the position of the firstborn son carries even greater significance. The firstborn son held a unique role, particularly in Jewish families. He ranked highest after his father and carried the weight of the father's authority. He was responsible for the oversight and well-being of the family (Gen. 49:3). For his extra leadership responsibility, he received an extra portion of his father's inheritance (Gen. 25:29–34; Deut. 21:17).

The firstborn son served as the representative of all the offspring of the family. Israel was figuratively called God's firstborn (Ex. 4:22). When Pharaoh stubbornly refused to release Israel, the Lord killed all the firstborn sons in Egypt except those who had been redeemed by the blood of a lamb. From then on, every firstborn male of the Israelites had to be redeemed (Ex. 11:4–7; 13:11–15). The oldest brother represented all his brothers and sisters. His redemption signified the redemption of them all.

Jot down some words to describe how you feel when you consider the fact that the male was the firstborn of mankind. (Resentful? Perplexed? Dismissive?)

_____

_____

Being firstborn doesn't indicate that the male is better than the female. In fact, it has nothing at all to do with the merits of the human male. The symbolism reflects and points to something far more significant.

Look up the following verses. Draw lines to match the titles of Christ on the left with the correct reference on the right:

Firstborn among
Many Brothers   **Colossians 1:15**

The Firstborn
(Only Begotten Son of God)   **Colossians 1:18**

Firstborn from the Dead   **Romans 8:29**

Firstborn of All Creation   **Hebrews 1:5–6**

Jesus Christ is THE Firstborn. He is the eternal Son of God, the firstborn of all creation. Scripture explains that this means He preceded creation and therefore has authority over everything that was created (Col. 1:15–20). As eternal firstborn, Christ defines the position of firstborn. The position and role of the firstborn male in Hebrew culture points to Christ's position and role, as does the position of husbands in marriage. It's all about Jesus Christ.

Summarize the responsibilities that accompany the position of firstborn male:

_____

_____

The human male was the firstborn of the human race. He carried the weight of responsibility for the oversight and well-being of the human family. He was the representative. God placed the mantle of leadership squarely on his shoulders. The New Testament attests to the fact that the male's firstborn status was significant, and that it has on-going implications for male leadership in the home and in the church (1 Tim. 2:13).

Again, this has nothing to do with the merits, worth, or superiority of the human male; it has everything to do with displaying the glory of God and the nature of Christ's relationship to His church (see Col. 1:18).

God created the male to be the "man of the house," the head of his household, to point to the relationship Jesus has with the church, which is the household of God (1 Tim. 3:15).

Read Ephesians 5:23–25 in the margin. How does the world's distorted concept of males being the "man of the house" differ from the example of Christ?

_____

_____

How do you think male-female relationships would be affected if men were to fulfill their firstborn responsibility to emulate Christ in the way they interact with women?

_____

_____

> "FOR THE HUSBAND IS THE HEAD OF THE WIFE EVEN AS CHRIST IS THE HEAD OF THE CHURCH, HIS BODY, AND IS HIMSELF ITS SAVIOR. . . . HUSBANDS, LOVE YOUR WIVES, AS CHRIST LOVED THE CHURCH AND GAVE HIMSELF UP FOR HER."
> Ephesians 5:23–25

king of the castle?

> "Those who are considered rulers of the Gentiles lord it over them, and their great ones exercise authority over them. But it shall not be so among you. But whoever would be great among you must be your servant, and whoever would be first among you must be slave of all. For even the Son of Man came not to be served but to serve, and to give his life as a ransom for many."
>
> **Mark 10:42–45**

The mound of snow on the playground was perfect for the game. At the red-bricked grade school I (Mary) attended in Canada, it was a favorite at recess time. When the bell rang, the first boy or girl to make it to the top got to be "king." The rest of us gathered at the base of the pile, waiting a turn to challenge the king's position. One by one, we'd storm up the hill and wrestle its occupant.

After a short scuffle, one child would prevail and the other would come tumbling down—arms and legs flailing—mitts, scarf, and hat covered in clumps of frosty white crystals. With upraised arms, the child who managed to stay on top would then exercise his or her bragging rights: "I'm the king of the castle, and you're the dirty rascal! NAH-nah-nah-NAH-nah!" the victor would taunt.

"King of the Castle" is a child's game. But sadly, it reflects some warped ideas that many adults have about authority. Authoritative positions are regarded as the best and most enviable positions. Everyone wants to be "king." The king is higher. The king is better. The king has more power. The king dominates. The king does whatever he wants. He gets all the perks. Everyone serves him. He looks down on others, bosses them around, lords it over them, and arrogantly forces them to cater to his every whim. The king couldn't care less about his minions. Compared to him, they're just dirty rascals. "NAH-nah-nah-NAH-nah!"

This skewed perspective of authority helps explain why so many people bristle at the suggestion that God assigns men to positions of authority within marriage and the church. But Jesus sharply rebuked His disciples for viewing authority as the right to dominate or to further one's personal interests. According to Him, this is a sinful perversion of what authority is all about.

Read Mark 10:35–45. In the space below, summarize Christ's perspective on how a person in authority should (and should NOT) view his or her position.

_____

_____

How does the life of Christ model a right view of authority?

_____

_____

   In answer to James and John's request for an esteemed place in God's kingdom, Jesus taught that true greatness comes by serving, not by selfishly seeking a position of authority. No one has an inherent right to claim a position of authority. The Father assigns such positions (Rom. 13:1). Jesus knew this. Even Christ's authority was delegated to Him by God the Father (Matt. 28:18).

   The Bible teaches that all authority rightfully belongs to God. Any legitimate authority people wield is delegated to them by God, and they must answer to Him for the way they use it. Authority is not to be used for personal gain. It's not about displaying personal power. It's about obediently serving the God who assigned you to serve in such a position—the very attitude demonstrated by Christ Himself.

   Jesus taught that authority is not about rights; it's about responsibility. It's not about getting; it's about giving. It's not about selfishness; it's about selflessness. It's not me-focused; it's other-focused. It's not the right to demand service; it's the responsibility to provide it. Authority is a position of weighty responsibility that demands radical obedience to the One from whom all authority flows. Greater authority demands greater responsibility. Scripture warns that those in such positions will be "judged with greater strictness" (James 3:1).

   Jesus wanted His disciples to grasp that true greatness isn't determined by how high up a person is on the pecking order. It has nothing to do with how much power a person wields. Rather, it has everything to do with how well a person humbly submits to God and serves others.

How does Christ's view on authority counter the idea of wives being squelched, dominated, or abused by their husbands—or men using positions of authority for personal gain?

_____

_____

Do you think God unfairly "favors" men or diminishes women by giving men a position of authority in the home? Explain.

_____

_____

What do you think it would be like to be under the authority of someone who loved and served you as Jesus loves and serves the church?

_____

_____

man up!

There's a crisis in manhood today. Over the past few years, an increasing number of secular sources have drawn attention to the subject in articles such as "The End of Men," "The Decline of Males," "The Death of Macho," books with titles like *Is There Anything Good about Men?,* and *Manning Up: How the Rise of Women Has Turned Men into Boys.*

This publishing trend reveals that society is keenly feeling the disintegration of manhood. There's a growing recognition that males aren't thriving. Today's cultural, ideological, and economic environment does not bring out the best in them. Even people who aren't followers of Christ are calling for guys to "man up" and be men.

According to the Bible, maleness and femaleness are essential, not peripheral, to our personhood. Sadly, in an attempt to promote the equality of men and women, our culture has depreciated the unique significance of who God created us to be. As a result, we now have a whole generation that has little if any sense of the beauty, value, and meaning of their manhood or womanhood.

As Pastor John Piper says, "Confusion over the meaning of sexual personhood today is epidemic. The consequence of this confusion is not a free and happy harmony among gender-free persons relating on the basis of abstract competencies. The consequence rather is more divorce, more homosexuality, more sexual abuse, more promiscuity, more social awkwardness, and more emotional distress and suicide that come with the loss of God-given identity."[3]

> "THIS DEPRECIATION OF MALE AND FEMALE PERSONHOOD IS A GREAT LOSS. IT IS TAKING A TREMENDOUS TOLL ON GENERATIONS OF YOUNG MEN AND WOMEN WHO DO NOT KNOW WHAT IT MEANS TO BE A MAN OR A WOMAN."
>
> —John Piper[2]

All this week we've been studying God's design for man. God created man with a unique responsibility to lead, provide, and protect. This does not mean that man gets to be king-of-the-castle, or to assume a more favorable position than woman. But it does mean that leadership, provision, protection, and responsible initiative are central and indispensable to what God created man to be. John Piper's definition of masculinity summarizes it well:

> *At the heart of mature masculinity is a sense of benevolent responsibility to lead, provide for and protect women in ways appropriate to a man's differing relationships.*[4]

In other words, the way a man relates to a wife, sister, daughter, colleague, or friend will differ, but all those relationships are informed and influenced who he is as a man. Masculinity means that he accepts a chivalrous responsibility to offer appropriate guidance, provision, and protection to the women in his life.

As you reflect on this week's study on biblical manhood, what are some of the things you appreciate about God's divine design for men?

_____

_____

Make a list of some of the men God has placed in your life—father, brothers, husband, sons, pastor, employer, coworkers, friends, etc. Ask the Lord to bless these men and to give them grace to be the men He created them to be. Thank the Lord for the men on your list who demonstrate the heart and character of Christ by being faithful providers and protectors and exercising authority with humility.

_____

_____

_____

_____

drawing it out, drawing it in . . .

snips & snails

process

The video for Week Two will help you process this week's lessons. You'll find this week's video, a downloadable outline/listening guide, and many more resources at www.TrueWoman101.com/week2.

ponder

Think about the following questions. Discuss them with your friends, family, and/or small group:

1. How does Hollywood typically portray men? Do you think this portrayal is accurate and fair?

2. Why do you think God created man first rather than creating the sexes at the same time? What implication does this have for the meaning of manhood?

3. God assigned the man responsibility to *work* and *keep* (see Gen. 2:15). What does this mean? In what way is this responsibility unique to manhood? Can you identify a time when a male friend or family member exemplified this bent? What do you think happens to men when they are absolved of this responsibility?

4. What does it mean to be the "man of the house"? What does it not mean? What exactly does it mean for a male to "man up"?

5. Do you think God's design for men benefits or harms women? Do you feel as though it favors men over women? Why or why not?

6. What are some ways in which women undermine manhood? What are some constructive ways in which we can affirm and encourage men to be men?

personalize

Use the following lined page to journal. Write down what you learned this week. Record your comments, a favorite verse, or a concept or quote that was particularly helpful or meaningful to you. Compose a prayer, letter, or poem. Jot down notes from the video or your small group session. Express your heart response to what you have studied. Personalize this week's lessons in the way that will best help you apply them to your life.

personalize it

sugar and spice

The Powerpuff Girls stormed onto TV screens in 1998, and instantly became the most highly rated animated series in the history of the Cartoon Network. This animated show was widely lauded by both young and old alike. It's not difficult to see that it had an underlying agenda. It sought to redefine traditional ideas about manhood and womanhood and turn gender roles upside down.

In the opening sequence, a bumbling professor attempts to create the perfect little girl using the traditional mixture of sugar, spice, and everything nice. But he spills "Chemical X" into the mixture, and fortuitously creates "super girls" who have superpowers of flight, superstrength, super speed, invulnerability, X-ray vision, super senses, heat vision, and energy projection.

The Powerpuff Girls spend their time fighting evil villains—most of whom are males. The highest and greatest villain of all—the epitome of evil—is a red-skinned, immortal devil-like creature called "HIM." HIM has a bad case of female envy. He speaks in a falsetto voice and cross-dresses in black thigh-high boots and a woman's red jacket and skirt with pink tulle at the collar and hemline.

In one of the most popular episodes, the Powerpuff Girls fight against their male counterparts, the Rowdyruff Boys, who were created using snips (armpit hair), snails (escargot), and a puppy dog's tail—plus a little water from the jailhouse toilet as a Chemical

X stand-in. The three boys personify the three evil traits of sexism, male chauvinism, and misogyny (girl hating). They exist only to destroy the Powerpuff Girls.

Initially, the Powerpuff Girls defeat the Rowdyruff Boys by giving them some sugar (their kisses). But when HIM resurrects the Boys to be even bigger and kiss-resistant, the Girls need to find another way to fight them. By chance, they discover that a boy's size diminishes whenever his masculinity is threatened. With that, the Girls emasculate the Boys by embarrassing them, mocking them, and insulting them. By attacking their manhood, the Boys are cut down to size and defeated.

The Powerpuff Girls may be just cartoon characters, but they reflect ideas about manhood and womanhood that are common in this day and age: Women are the powerful ones. Women are the smart ones. Women are the ones who need to save men from themselves. The media portrays men as either evil, aggressive abusers, or as inferior, bumbling, incompetent fools. Women are the ones who need to be strong, take charge, and be in control. As the modern-day kindergarten chant goes, "Girls Rule and Guys Drool!"

The Powerpuff Girls was but one of the media's countless bids to change the definition of what little (and big) girls are made of. While the traditional, 1950s image of womanhood didn't necessarily get it all right, it did affirm that men and women had distinct, unique roles that were vital to the function of the family and the good of society. But the women's movement changed all that. It infused women with the idea that we have the right to decide for ourselves what it means to be a woman.

Last week, we had a look at Genesis to determine what little boys are made of. This week we'll do the same for little girls. As God was intentional in His creation of men, so our design as women is not accidental or arbitrary. We were uniquely designed by our Creator with specific purposes in mind.

As we consider those purposes, keep in mind that the world does not affirm God's plan, and it tells us in a thousand different ways why we should not accept it either. All of us have been influenced by the world's message to greater or lesser degrees. So as we consider our God-created design, you may find yourself bristling at times, when His plan runs counter to the image of womanhood promoted by our culture.

That's why it's so important to approach this matter by first bowing our hearts before Him and saying "*Yes, Lord!*"

Before you dive into this week's lesson, why don't you take a moment to do just that? Acknowledge that He is God and you are not. Affirm that His ways are right and good. Ask Him to show you His ways and to give you grace to embrace them and to live out His design for your life. →

it's a girl!

On several occasions, I (Nancy) have had a young couple living in my home when they found out they were expecting a child. The excitement of that announcement was always followed by the anticipation of finding out whether the baby would be a "he" or a "she."

Partway through her second pregnancy, one young friend of mine had an ultrasound and was told she was carrying a baby boy. Through the rest of the pregnancy, Maggie and Brent eagerly prepared to welcome a second son into their family. Imagine their astonishment when Maggie first looked down at the newborn baby she was holding in her arms and said, "Wait . . . is that a . . . *girl??*" It was indeed! (The shocked parents had to scramble, as they had not even considered a name for a girl and did not own anything "pink"!)

"It's a Boy!" or "It's a Girl!" is usually the first fact announced at the birth of a baby. Some people claim that sex ought to be of no consequence to a person's identity or role. But author Elisabeth Elliot disagrees. She published a compilation of notes to her daughter on the meaning of womanhood, in a book called *Let Me Be a Woman*. In reflecting on the meaning of femaleness, Elisabeth wrote to her daughter:

> *Yours is the body of a woman. What does it signify? Is there invisible meaning in its visible signs—the softness, the smoothness, the lighter bone and muscle structure, the breasts, the womb? Are they utterly unrelated to what you yourself are? Isn't your identity intimately bound up with these material forms?*[1]

What do you think Elisabeth was trying to telling her daughter?

I (Mary) want you to do a fun exercise that I sometimes do with the gals in a seminary class I teach on biblical womanhood. Stand up and drop your arms down by the side of your body. Keeping your arms relaxed; turn your hands so that your palms face forward. Do you see that the lower part of your arm does not line up straight with your upper arm? It veers off at the elbow, away from your body, at about a twenty to thirty degree angle.

Next, I want you to find a male and ask him to assume the same position. You'll see that his arm is fairly straight. His lower arm only veers off about five to ten degrees. Compared to a man's arm, your arm is markedly crooked. (It's true!) That's because God made you with a special carrying angle! The bent in your arm allows you to cradle and nurse a child. The differing carrying angle is what makes it awkward for you to throw a football, and less natural for a guy to hold a baby.

When I studied rehab medicine, I learned that besides the obvious anatomical differences, there are a myriad of physiological and psychological differences between men and women. Men have 50 percent greater total muscle mass, based on weight, than do women. A woman who is the same size as her male counterpart is generally only 80 percent as strong. A woman's body is much more efficient at storing energy (fat) to give her reserves for pregnancy and lactation. Men have larger hearts and lungs and greater amounts of red blood cells. When a man is jogging at about 50 percent of his capacity, a woman will need to work at over 70 percent of her capacity to keep up.

The male brain is larger than the female brain, but women have four times as many neurons connecting the right and left sides. Men tend to process better in the left hemisphere of the brain while women tend to process equally well between the two hemispheres. This difference explains why men generally have better spatial and mathematical abilities and approach problem-solving from a task-oriented perspective, while women are generally more perceptive, more attuned to feelings, better at communication, and more creative.

Men tend to respond to stress with a "fight or flight" response while women respond with a "tend and befriend" strategy. That means that women increase their focus inward on family and children (tending) and form strong group bonds (befriending) in times of difficulty, while men increase their outward focus in order to deal with the threat. The reason for these different reactions is rooted in differing hormones.

The female body produces a large quantity of a hormone called oxytocin, which promotes bonding and affiliation and enhances maternal instinct. The male body produces large quantities of testosterone, which creates the push to advance, take risks, guard, and conquer.[2]

In the space below, list some differences you have noticed in how males and females act and interact:

_____

_____

Elisabeth Elliot wanted her daughter to understand that the differences in a woman's body testify to the fact that God created her to have a different role than man. She wanted her to take note of the "invisible meaning" of the visible signs.

Male-female differences are profound. A man's body is structured in such a way that he is the one who moves out and toward and has strength to give. A woman's body is structured in such a way that she is the one who welcomes, draws in, and has capacity to receive and nurture.

When the Lord presented the first man with his wife, the man burst out into a poem that expressed this fundamental difference:

> *Then the man said,*
> *"This at last is bone of my bones*
>   *and flesh of my flesh;*
> *she shall be called Woman,*
>   *because she was taken out of Man"* (Gen. 2:23).

In the verse above, circle the words "Woman" and "Man."

In Hebrew, the name with which the male identified himself was *ish*, while his name for woman was *ishshah*. This appears to be a clever and profound play on words. The sound of these two Hebrew words is nearly identical—*ishshah* merely adds a feminine ending—but the two words have a complementary meaning. Many scholars believe that *ish* comes from the root meaning "strength," while *ishshah* comes from the root meaning "soft." [3]

Fill in the blanks with the corresponding meaning:

  Woman = Hebrew *"ishshah"* = _____

  Man = Hebrew *"ish"* = _____

Based on what you learned last week about God's design for man, in what ways does He want man to exercise "strength"?

_____

_____

What do you think the term "soft" implies about who God created woman to be?

_____

_____

not one of the guys

S *Softness is at the core of what it means to be a woman.* If you look up the dictionary definition of "soft," you'll find that it means not hard; yielding readily to touch, flexible, pliable; delicate, graceful; not loud; quietly pleasant; calm, gentle, kind, tender, compassionate, and sympathetic.

The New Testament uses a similar word—"weaker"—to reinforce that women are the softer, more vulnerable ones. This does not at all imply that

women are inferior to men. However, women are physically and emotionally more tender, and are thus more susceptible to being hurt. According to 1 Peter 3:7, God expects men to honor them for this beautiful feminine trait. He warns men not to treat women like "one of the guys." God expects men to handle women like Swarovski crystal, and not like Bridgestone tires!

The world has programmed women to disdain "softness." We are encouraged to be tough and even hard. But the world's model of womanhood misses out on the beauty of who God created us to be as women.

What negative reaction or fears might the thought of being considered the "soft" ones evoke in some women?

_____

_____

What benefits and blessings could result from women embracing this mind-set?

_____

_____

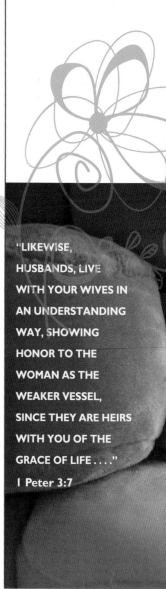

"LIKEWISE, HUSBANDS, LIVE WITH YOUR WIVES IN AN UNDERSTANDING WAY, SHOWING HONOR TO THE WOMAN AS THE WEAKER VESSEL, SINCE THEY ARE HEIRS WITH YOU OF THE GRACE OF LIFE . . . ."
1 Peter 3:7

"Then the LORD God said, 'It is not good that the man should be alone; I will make him a helper fit for him.' ... But for [the man] there was not found a helper fit for him."

Genesis 2:18–20

"For man was not made from woman, but woman from man. Neither was man created for woman, but woman for man."

I Corinthians 11:8–9

Most women enjoy a good chick flick. By chick flick we mean a story that taps into the depths and complexities of human relationships. Something like those classic favorites "Little Women" and "Pride and Prejudice." A chick flick contains romance and chivalry, or depicts family relationships or bonds between friends. It includes multifaceted characters, rich dialogue, and a satisfying relational ending. In contrast to the male-tale, a chick flick does not require that one single thing in the movie blows up.

One of the happy benefits of having a married oldest son is that I (Mary) now have a daughter-in-law. That means I have a kindred spirit when it comes to casting a vote as to which movie gets the nod on family movie night. For far too many years, I was over-ruled by the men and their preference for action scenes, fast cars, guns, blood, and battle. I'll never forget the first time Jacqueline was in on the movie selection process, and my son advocated that his new bride make the choice. Much to my delight, we wound up plugging a tear-jerking, sappy chick flick into the Blu-Ray.

My two unmarried sons didn't last long. After about fifteen minutes they disappeared like our dog's dinner. But the married men hung in there. (Greater love hath no man than to watch a chick flick with his woman!) Jacqueline and I sat side by side on the love seat, riveted. We were both dabbing our eyes with Kleenex when we heard a muffled sob come from the adjacent couch. As I

reached over to pass the box, a second sound rumbled from Brent's throat. But it clearly indicated that he wasn't crying. He was snoring. He was fast asleep. And so was Clark, whose semi-comatose frame was propped up on cushions on the floor.

Not one male in our household lasted to the end of that movie. Not one. Even the dog fell asleep and joined the male chorus of sawing logs. But in Jacqueline's and my estimation, it was a fabulous movie! And afterward we told the men (who groaned and dramatically rolled their eyeballs) that we would both love to see it again.

The reason so many women are drawn toward chick flicks is that God created us to be highly relational beings. Genesis 2 tells us that God created the female "for him"—that is, for the male. First Corinthians 11:9 reinforces that woman was created "for the man" and not the other way around. According to Genesis 2, this means she was designed to assist him in fulfilling his God-given calling, as his support and helper. But the fact that she was created "for" the man also helps us understand what we know instinctively to be true—that the woman is inherently relational.

In the verses in the margin on the facing page, circle all the "for him/for man" phrases.

In the space below, jot down some words that describe how you think most women today would feel about the concept of the woman being made for the man:

_____

_____

For many women, on first hearing, the idea of woman being created "for" man may seem quite negative, since it appears to imply that he has license to use and abuse her at will. But the Scripture in no way supports such a concept.

Our negative reaction to having been created "for" man serves to highlight how far we've fallen from the original created order. When the first bride was presented to her husband, her heart was undoubtedly bursting with joy to have been created for him. She could not have felt more satisfied, for she was fulfilling the purpose for which she had been designed. She was made "from" the man, made "for" the man, and given as a gift "to" the man.

In Adam, joyfully receiving Eve as "bone of [his] bone" and "flesh of [his] flesh"—equal, yet different—Eve experienced the deep relational connection that she was created to enjoy, and for which women are hardwired to yearn.

Of course, woman's unique bent toward relationships doesn't mean that men aren't interested in or are incapable of forming deep bonds. But it does mean that women have a drive and capacity for relationships that is unique to what it means to be a woman.

As I (Nancy) am working on this book, 'tis the season for weddings. Several of my friends' children and one of our staff members are "tying the knot" within the space of a few weeks. It has been a sweet thing to observe, listen to, and talk and pray with these young women—each of them quite different—and to enjoy their sense that they have been created "for" the man they are marrying, that they are tailor-made for each other.

Sooner or later, of course (probably sooner than later), they will each discover that they are a sinner married to a sinner, which will at times cause them to compete with rather than complete each other, and so strain their relational connection. But they are starting out with the belief that God has fashioned them for each other and with a longing to love and be loved and to connect on a deep emotional level.

Being created "for someone" indicates that God created the female to be a highly relational creature. In contrast to the male, her identity isn't based on work nearly as much as on how well she connects and relates to others. *Forming deep relational bonds is at the core of what it means to be a woman.*

What evidences or examples can you think of that demonstrate that women are "hardwired" for relational connectedness?

_____

_____

The woman's drive to relationally connect is a powerful one. In yesterday's lesson we saw that the female body produces a high level of a hormone called oxytocin, which promotes bonding and emotional connection. Woman was created with a built-in desire to be relationally affiliated with others. She wants to bond. She is drawn toward romance, and also toward forming other deep, satisfying relationships—with sisters, brothers, children, neighbors, friends, or colleagues.

Even the anatomy of a woman's body indicates that she was created "for" something. There's a "space" within her that is shaped to receive. God created the woman's body with a place "for" the man's body.

But it's important to understand that this physical reality is merely an earthly illustration that points to a far greater eternal spiritual truth. Ultimately, the fact that woman was created "for" man doesn't mean that every woman needs to get "hitched" to a man. Nor does it mean that the deepest longings of a woman's heart can be fully met by a man. Rather, it's an object lesson that's meant to teach us about God. It's a reflection of the eternal relationship for which we all (both men and women) were formed.

Woman being created "for" man reminds us that the church-bride was created "for" Jesus Christ. A woman's pull toward romance and relationships is a picture of every person's need to connect with Him. King David expressed it well. He likened his soul's thirst for God to the "panting" of a deer for water.

Sadly, most women don't understand that Christ is the only one who can ultimately satisfy the deepest yearnings of a woman's heart. So they become disillusioned when their husbands don't meet all of their needs, or they go through a series of revolving-door relationships, looking for a man who will.

I (Mary) will never forget praying with Jenna, a woman who had burned through five marriages—yes, five—just like the woman Jesus met at the well. Jenna's fifth marriage had recently disintegrated, and she wanted me to pray for her to find another man—"the right one." "I just want to find someone who'll fill the void in my heart!" she sobbed on my shoulder.

I didn't pray for Jenna to find another husband. There's no man on the face of the earth that could ever quench her deepest longings. Jenna's desire—and the desire in every woman's heart—can only be fully satisfied in a relationship with Jesus Christ. That's the relationship to which all of our womanly longings point.

Describe a season of your life in which you have struggled with unsatisfied longings for relational connectedness. How have you tried to fulfill that longing?

_____

_____

How can unfulfilled longings ("thirst") point us to the ultimate Relationship for which we were created?

_____

_____

steel magnolia

"And the rib that the LORD God had taken from the man he made into a woman and brought her to the man. Then the man said, '...she shall be called Woman, because she was taken out of Man'"

Genesis 2:22–23

"The man called his wife's name Eve, because she was the mother of all living."

Genesis 3:20

"Let your adorning be the hidden person of the heart with the imperishable beauty of a gentle and quiet spirit, which in God's sight is very precious."

I Peter 3:4

For several years I (Nancy) lived part-time in Little Rock, Arkansas. Having spent most of my life in the North, I so enjoyed the many plants and trees indigenous to the more temperate Southern climate. One of my favorite springtime sights in the South was the magnificent magnolia trees, with their large, glossy leaves and huge white blossoms.

The magnolia has been associated in art, specifically in Chinese art, as a symbol of feminine beauty and sweetness. This fragrant flower is often used in wedding bouquets to represent the purity and dignity of the bride. This is particularly the case in the South, where "Steel Magnolia" is used as a popular phrase to describe the delicate yet strong nature of Southern women.

That phrase reflects something of the essence of true womanhood. The image melds beauty with perseverance, softness with backbone, delicacy with durability, sweetness with stamina, and gentleness with gumption.

So far in Genesis, we've seen that God created woman to be the "soft" one, and that He created her with a deep desire to bond and connect. In today's lesson, you'll see that a woman's softness also involves her having a sweet, amenable spirit—one that joyfully responds and defers to others. When her life is under the control of the Spirit of God, this responsiveness is accompanied by a steadfast determination to be receptive to the right influences. A heart that is resolute to respond to God first and foremost puts steel into the magnolia.

Read Genesis 2:22–23 and 3:20 in the margin. How did the female come by her name?

_____

_____

What does this indicate about the nature of the relationship between the first husband and wife?

_____

_____

As you reflect on the Genesis account, how do you think the woman responded to being named by her husband?

_____

_____

Last week, when we looked at Adam going through the paces of the *name-that-animal* exercise, we learned that to name something is to exercise authority over it. Adam understood his God-given responsibility to lead, provide, protect, and serve his household. So when God presented him with a wife, he immediately stepped up to the plate to serve her by providing her with a befitting name. Do you think she beamed in response? The Bible doesn't say. But even more telling than how she responded to Adam's initiative is how she undoubtedly *didn't* respond.

Eve's reaction is markedly different than the way women today are trained to respond when men take the lead. If Eve would have had even the slightest feminist notion bouncing around her head, she would not have been happy about Adam unilaterally giving her a name.

She would've placed her hands squarely on her hips and told him, "I think I'll name myself, thank you very much!" Or, she might have insisted on a hyphenated

name. Or spouted off, "What's good for the goose is good for the gander!" and insisted she and Adam both contribute fifty-fifty to each other's names: she would go by "Ms. Wom-Man" if he would go by "Mr. Man-Wom." Their male children could be named after him and their female children after her. That sounds way fairer, doesn't it?

We suspect the reason the Bible doesn't record Eve's response to Adam's naming is because she responded just as God expected she would—with joy

and deference. She responded in a way that was natural and appropriate. It was the wholehearted, happy response of a sinless bride to the leadership of her sinless groom. When God presented her to the man, Adam and Eve acted according to their God-given bents. He initiated. She responded. The pattern of their relationship reflected who God created them to be.

A woman is a relator. A woman is a responder. *Having a receptive, responsive spirit is at the core of what it means to be a woman*. A godly woman is an "*amen*able" woman—an agreeable woman. She says yes (amen!). She has a disposition that responds positively to others, and particularly to the initiative of godly men. She is "soft" and not obstinate about receiving direction. She is "leadable."

Scripture tells us that this womanly disposition is beautiful and of great worth to God. It finds its expression in married life through a wife's submission to her husband. But a soft, amenable disposition isn't just for married women. It's for women of all ages, regardless of marital status.

Do you feel that "responsiveness" is a positive or negative trait? Explain why.

_____

_____

I (Mary) gotta admit, at times in the past when I heard the words "soft" and "submissive," I had to fight against a caricature that came to mind. I would envision myself with a spray tan and fake eyelashes, drowning in bleached curls and cotton-candy-colored taffeta, sporting a bulging-eyed Chihuahua in my purse, and nodding yes to everything like a mindless bobble-head doll—in short, violating my personality and acting like a DITZ! The thought was as unappealing to me as the oatmeal slop I ate for breakfast this morning.

Naysayers would have us believe that biblical directives turn women into brain-dead, passive, weak-willed doormats who mindlessly acquiesce to the whims of thoughtless or controlling men. But nothing could be further from the truth.

Yes, God created women to be soft responders, but He also expects us to make wise, intentional, God-informed choices about what we respond to. God doesn't want His girls to be wilting, weak-willed, wimpy women. He doesn't violate our personalities. And He doesn't want us to be responsive to the wrong things!

That was Eve's downfall. Instead of seeking the advice of her husband, and being steadfast in faithfully responding to the Lord, she was responsive to the Serpent. As a result of being receptive to an influence that ran counter to God's ways, she was deceived and gave in to Satan's temptation.

The New Testament talks about some other women who didn't respond as God wanted them to but were "weak-willed."

Read 2 Timothy 3:6–7 in the margin on page 78. What three characteristics of weak-willed women do you see in this passage?

1. _____

2. _____

3. _____

Can you think of any illustrations of how "weak-willed" women might be responsive to the control of ungodly influences?

_____

_____

The Lord created His girls to have responsive spirits. Women are responders. Responding is in our nature. We will either respond to good or we will respond to evil. We will either respond to truth or be swayed by lies. If we don't establish the practice of receiving and responding to God's Word, we will be more vulnerable to be receptive and responsive to the wrong kinds of men, ideas, or counsel.

In the space below, list some of the wrong kinds of influences you've seen women (perhaps including yourself) be responsive to.

_____

_____

How could you cultivate a heart that is even more soft and responsive to Christ and His Word?

_____

_____

nesting

"...train the young women to [be]... working at home."

Titus 2:4–5

"So I would have younger widows marry, bear children, manage their households, and give the adversary no occasion for slander."

I Timothy 5:14

"She looks well to the ways of her household."

Proverbs 31:27

There's nothing quite as comforting during a harsh Canadian winter as crawling under the protective cover of my (Mary's) cozy goose down duvet. The mercury here has been known to drop down to minus 48 degrees Celsius (-55° F) at night—minus 58 Celsius (-78° F) with wind chill. Edmonton has at times rivaled the Arctic as the coldest place on earth. But my downy cover is a place of repose. It's like being cradled in a layer of soft, warm contentment, hidden and sheltered from the cold cruel elements outside.

Down duvets are without equal in bedding warmth and comfort—particularly the coveted eiderdown, filled with feathers collected from the nests of the Arctic Sea eider. An eiderdown duvet is so incredibly light-weight and cozy that it's like being tucked into a delicate warm cloud of bliss. There's nothing like it! And in my mind, there's no better illustration for today's lesson.

The mother eider, like other female birds, plucks the soft, delicate down from deep near her heart. She uses feathers drawn from her most intimate parts to line her nest, and thus transforms a base of twigs into a snug, warm, soothing, comforting place—ready to welcome and nurture life. Though the male often helps, the female oversees nest construction, and it is from her breast that the soft, downy comfort comes.

This beautiful nesting practice of female birds mirrors the precious capability that God gave women. He created women with a remarkable capacity to create an environment conducive to welcoming and nurturing life. Women are specially equipped to make a house into a home. We are nurturers. We create a fertile place. We birth life. We (so to speak) pluck soft, downy feathers from our hearts to line our nests, so our broods can hatch and flourish.

According to the verses in the margin, what is one of the top priorities of a godly woman?

The Lord created man out in the field that he would one day work (not until after his creation was he placed in the garden). The location of man's creation seems to be connected to his distinct sphere of responsibility. The woman, on the other hand, wasn't created out in the field. She was created within the boundaries of the garden—the "home" where God had placed her husband. This detail is intriguing, since Scripture indicates that managing the household is a woman's distinct sphere of responsibility.

Again, please don't misunderstand. A woman has a "distinct" responsibility to manage the home, not an "exclusive" responsibility to do everything in it. This does not imply that husbands and other members of the household cannot or should not contribute. But it does indicate that just as God wired man to be connected to work in a way woman is not, so He wired woman to be connected to home and relationships in a way man is not.

The Bible teaches that God created woman with a distinctively feminine "bent" for the home. "Working at home" is on its *Top Ten* list of important things that older women need to teach the younger ones (Titus 2:4–5). Scripture encourages young women to "manage their households" (1 Tim. 5:14). It praises the woman who "looks well to the ways [affairs] of her household" (Prov. 31:27). And it casts in a negative light women whose hearts are inclined away from the home—those whose "feet" are not centered there (Prov. 7:11).

What do you think it means for a woman to look well to the ways of her household?

_____

_____

How might this calling to manage the home be applied by single women?

_____

_____

nesting instinct

We've all heard about the nesting instinct and how it especially kicks in sometime around the fifth month of a woman's pregnancy. Preparing a room for the baby, stocking up with baby supplies, and sorting the baby's clothes over and over again are common nesting behaviors. Women also tell stories of washing all the windows, cleaning all the floors, or organizing all their kitchen cupboards shortly before they give birth.

This burst of home-focused energy is likely due to an increase in prolactin, sometimes referred to as the *mothering* or *nesting* hormone— or perhaps due to a change in the balance between the female hormones estrogen and progesterone.[4]

Mothering and nesting hormones exist at higher levels when a woman is pregnant, but they are always an important part of a woman's makeup. That's because *creating a place to beget and nurture life is at the core of what it means to be a woman.*

How has our culture devalued the woman's natural, God-created affinity for the home?

_____

_____

What are some ways a childless woman might welcome and nurture life?

_____

_____

Contemporary Western culture greatly devalues what happens in the home. It views homemaking as a conglomeration of meaningless tasks such as cleaning toilets, scrubbing floors, folding laundry . . . things a monkey could be trained to do. But every woman knows that creating a home is about much more than the sum of the tasks it involves.

Creating a home is not about checking tasks off a list or about filling a house with material possessions—it's ultimately about people. It's about creating a warm, nurturing, orderly, stable place that promotes well-being and fosters physical, emotional, mental, and spiritual growth. It's about welcoming others in. It's about ministering to the soul. It's about community. It's about cultivating relationships. And that's something God has particularly equipped women to do.

When we create a home, we provide a "cover" where family and friends can retreat and be sheltered from the cold cruel world outside. A place where they'll feel cocooned and cradled in a comfy cloud of love. A place where they can rest and recharge from the daily grind. A place where they can flourish. A place that foreshadows the welcome believers will receive in heaven. A place that calls and beckons them "Home."

As an expression of my heart for creating a "nest," I (Mary) have baked cookies for my sons' school events, when it would have been easier to just give them five bucks to pick up a pack at the grocery store. I crochet lacy snowflakes for my Christmas tree, even though I could buy them at the craft mart. I put time and effort into home décor, even though I could just hire someone to buy pictures and hang them on the walls. I invite people over for a home-cooked meal, even though I could just take them out to a restaurant.

There's no "checklist" of what "godly nesting" looks like. Because I (Nancy) am single and have full-time ministry responsibilities, the way I "create a home" looks different than it does for Mary. But I often invite out-of-town guests to stay in my home, when it would be simpler to have them stay in a hotel. I like to place fresh flowers in the guest room, along with a handwritten note of welcome. I have hosted many Bible studies and staff gatherings in my home, when it would have been more convenient to have met elsewhere.

Why go to all this trouble? Because in doing so we give of ourselves. And in giving, we nurture others and facilitate their growth.

As we women serve in these and other ways, we are like the mother eider. We give what only a woman can give. We pluck the soft, delicate "down" from deep near our hearts and use those feathers to line our nests. We transform stark twigs into a snug, warm, soothing, comforting place. Every woman is created to "mother" and "nest." Even if she never bears biological children, every woman is created to welcome, beget, and nurture life.

What are some relationships God has given you, in which you can welcome, beget, and nurture life?

_____

_____

How can your home be used as a place to nurture life? (Your "home" may be a house, apartment, double-wide trailer, dorm room, prison cell, hospital room, or retirement home!)

_____

_____

crook in my arm

The visible, physical design of our bodies points to invisible, spiritual aspects of our unique, divine design as women. Our flesh is smooth and our bodies curvaceous. We have a womb. We have a crook in our arm. Our physical makeup indicates that we were created to welcome, receive, respond, beget, and nurture.

That doesn't mean that every woman will be married and bear children. It doesn't mean we will act the same, dress the same, or make the same choices. God has given us unique personalities, gifts, and strengths. And our life circumstances vary greatly. True Womanhood will look different from one woman to another and from one life season to another. God doesn't give us a cookie-cutter pattern to follow. A woman who loves sports and riding motorbikes can be just as womanly as a "girlie-girl" who loves sparkles or lace.

Nevertheless, Scripture does present some universal truths about the meaning of womanhood. So far, in our study of Genesis, we've seen several elements that are at the core of what it means to be a woman:

- *Softness*
- *Forming deep relational bonds*
- *Having a welcoming, responsive spirit*
- *Creating a place to beget and nurture life*

We love John Piper's description of the heart of biblical womanhood:

At the heart of mature femininity is a freeing disposition to affirm, receive and nurture strength and leadership from worthy men in ways appropriate to a woman's differing relationships.[5]

Woman is the soft one—the relater, the responder, the nurturer. Genesis uses a term to summarize what God had in mind for creating her this way.

> "Then the LORD God said, 'It is not good that the man should be alone; I will make a helper fit for him.'"
>
> **Genesis 2:18**

Fill in the blanks to complete the phrase describing what the Lord created when He created woman:

"a _____ _____ for him"

How do you feel about woman being the "helper"?

_____

_____

What do you think the woman was created to help man do?

_____

_____

Some people react negatively to the idea that woman was created to be man's helper. They assume that this relegates her to a secondary role, where the woman is the servant and the man is the one who gets served: she is the one who unilaterally helps him. She "helps" him by picking up his dirty clothes and cooking his meals, for example. While a woman can help her husband domestically, this view of the role of *helper* misses the essential point.

Contrary to what some have suggested, "helper" is not a demeaning term that indicates a lesser status, or the type of help that assists in a trivial way. The Hebrew word (*ezer*) is a powerful one. It's most often used with reference to the Lord being our helper (Pss. 33:20; 72:12). An "*ezer*" provides help that is absolutely and utterly indispensable.

In order to understand the implications of the woman's "helper" design, we need to consider what woman is to "help" man do. The male was created to bring glory to God—and to serve Him (rather than himself). This is man's ultimate purpose. So that rules out the idea that God created woman to help the man cater to his own selfish ends. No. God created a helper to assist the man in fulfilling his ultimate purpose. Woman helps man glorify God in a way he could not do if she did not exist.

At creation, the Lord's stated goal was to expand His family—He wanted humans to "be fruitful and multiply." This is something the male could not do

without the female. Without woman's help, it would be impossible for the man to generate life. She has an indispensable role to play in helping him fulfill the purposes of God.

Woman is a helper to man in a similar manner to the way the church is a helper to Christ. The church helps Christ glorify God. Together, the church and Christ bear fruit. New life. New disciples. Together, they expand the family of God, and thus bring glory to the Father. Here again, the visible realm teaches us about the greater, unseen realities.

The union of husband and wife generates physical life. Likewise, the invisible union of Christ and the church generates spiritual life. In both the physical and the spiritual realm, the woman helps the man bring forth life.

The purpose of woman helping man isn't about exalting the man. It's really not about him (or her) at all. Her help contributes to the both of them achieving a greater, nobler eternal purpose that is far bigger and more significant than their own existence. She labors and serves alongside him for the same purpose for which he labors and serves. And what is that? The glory of God. Woman helps man achieve the purpose of exalting and displaying the jaw-dropping magnificence of the gospel of Jesus Christ.

If you are married, how well are you fulfilling your God-created design to be a helper to your husband?

In a broader sense, what are some ways women can be a help to men as we seek to glorify God together?

---

perfect match

God was the first Matchmaker. When He created woman, He created her to be the perfect mate. The first and foundational human relationship was a marriage—a union that was intended to reflect profound truths about the gospel. As we saw in Week One, men were created to reflect the strength, love, and self-sacrifice of Christ. Women were created to reflect the responsiveness, grace, and beauty of the bride He would one day redeem.

Scripture traces the differences in male-female roles and responsibilities back to the way things were in Eden before sin corrupted our relationships. Some would argue that relationships with role differences are inherently demeaning or abusive. But that's not what we observe in the first marriage. The relationship between the first man and woman was absolutely perfect. It was a paradise of love, unity, and joy, which we can now only faintly imagine.

This lesson on the creation of woman may have raised as many questions for you as it has answered. *What about women's rights? What implications does this have for the decisions I make about relationships, marriage, and children? How should this affect my approach to education, career, and employment? How can I cultivate a soft spirit without violating my personality or turning into a wimp? What if my marriage relationship feels more like hell than paradise? How do I live by God's design when others don't?*

By the end of this study you'll have more insight into how to think through these kinds of questions. It's one thing to understand God's ideal; it's another to apply it in a world that is broken and fractured by sin. Nevertheless, we hope that these first few weeks have opened your eyes to the meaning of true manhood and womanhood, and given you a glimpse into the beauty of His divine design!

This week we've considered several elements that are at the heart of what it means to be a woman:

- *Softness*
- *Forming deep relational bonds*
- *Having a welcoming, responsive spirit*
- *Creating a place to beget and nurture life*
- *Being a helper*

Which of these do you find the most challenging or difficult? Ask the Lord to mold you into a woman who reflects His heart and ways.

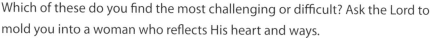

drawing it out, drawing it in . . .

sugar and spice

process

The video for Week Three will help you process this week's lessons. You'll find this week's video, a downloadable outline/listening guide, and many more resources at www.TrueWoman101.com/week3. Make sure and check it out!

ponder

Think about the following questions. Discuss them with your friends, family, and/or small group:

1. How does Hollywood typically portray women? What do you find attractive or unattractive about its portrayal?

2. What do the differences between male and female bodies suggest about what it means to be a man or woman?

3. Many believe that the Hebrew words for *man* and *woman* (Gen. 2:23) suggest that man is identified with "strength" and woman with "softness." What does this mean? Does the idea of "softness" repel or attract you? Why?

4. What's the difference between a "chick flick" and a "male tale" (movie)? What does this indicate about the natural bent of man and woman?

5. Do you view "responsiveness" as a positive or negative trait? Why? How do we remain "soft" but avoid becoming passive, weak-willed doormats?

6. How do you feel about the fact that God created woman with a distinctively feminine "bent" for the home? In what way is every woman created to "mother" and "nest"?

7. What aspect of God's design for womanhood do you find the most difficult? Why?

personalize:

Use the following lined page to journal. Write down what you learned this week. Record your comments, a favorite verse, or a concept or quote that was particularly helpful or meaningful to you. Compose a prayer, letter, or poem. Jot down notes from the video or your small group session. Express your heart response to what you have studied. Personalize this week's lessons in the way that will best help you apply them to your life.

personalize it

drawing it out,
drawing it in . . .

snake in my garden

Each year, when spring finally makes its appearance in Canada, I (Mary) enjoy taking a trip down to my local greenhouse to pick out some annual flowers for my backyard—petunias, geraniums, and marigolds for the sunny rock planters; pansies, impatiens, and begonias for the ones in the shade; lobelia and spiky dracaena to tuck into the pots; million bells for the hanging baskets … you get the picture. By midsummer, my backyard is usually overflowing with fragrance, color, and beauty. Except a few years ago. The summer the slugs invaded.

I fought valiantly. I tried slug bait, slug poison, drowning them in stale beer, trapping them in sawed-off soda bottles, warding them off with eggshell shards, and plugging up their bellies with oat bran, but it was a losing battle. They still turned my lovely blooms into Swiss cheese.

In the garden of Eden, Adam and Eve probably didn't need to fight off a slug invasion. But there was a far more nefarious enemy lurking in their garden—an enemy that wanted to ruin their relationship with God. This week, we'll be taking a look at the Serpent's strategy, how Eve fell for the deception, and how sin started to make Swiss cheese, first of her relationship with God, and then of the male-female relationship. And we'll see how those consequences have been passed down to every human being who has lived ever since.

At *Revive Our Hearts*, I (Nancy) get many letters from women (and some from men) who describe the impact of the Enemy's schemes on male-female relationships:

- *I am at the end of myself. My husband has fallen asleep in front of the TV for three years, and I am downright bitter and hateful, because he doesn't love me or hold me as a husband should. I am feeling weary and hateful, which I know is wrong; I slam doors and pout, but cannot tell him why I am so angry. Now he says he is tired of being mistreated. All he has done for years is yell and scream and scare me. So . . . I am the bad guy!?! I await God's answer to these prayer requests, but in the meantime I am angry and tired.*

- *I have emasculated my husband as a man and in his walk with the Lord because of my selfish, arrogant, manipulative, intimidating ways and words. How terribly, terribly wounded he is because of me.*

- [from a man] *I haven't been out with a REAL woman in many years. The reason is simple; I haven't found a REAL woman in years. The so-called modern woman is aggressive, controlling, rude, loud, overbearing, obnoxious, unfaithful, disrespectful . . . even women at church. I miss the strong but feminine, delicate, romantic, caring, loving, helpful, good mother, good companion, sentimental women of years gone by.*

God's enemy, Satan, works hard to make a mess of the beauty of our divine design. He fights to mar the splendor of what we were created to display. He does his utmost to prevent both male and female from showcasing God's amazing story.

There was a (literal) snake in Eve's garden. And sadly, her response meant that there would be a "snake" in the garden of every woman from that point on—that is to say, we would be a target of the schemes and temptations of God's archenemy, the Devil himself. That's the bad news.

The good news is that Scripture makes us wise to Satan's strategy and that the power of Jesus Christ enables us to fight back and defeat the Enemy. Over the next couple of weeks, you'll learn more about the Snake in your garden, how he seeks to destroy manhood, womanhood, marriage, and family, and how, by God's grace, we can reclaim the beauty of God's divine design. →

enemy in the gate

Helping people find the perfect mate is a billion-plus dollar industry in this country. Internet dating services, social net-working sites, and speed-dating events abound. There's even a matchmaking institute that provides training and certification for wannabe matchmakers. One popular reality show revolves around finding a perfect match for a bachelor. He's presented with a slate of dozens of eligible women. As the weeks go by, he narrows down his choice to one, and then proposes marriage. Sadly, the efforts of this show, like those of other matchmaking enterprises that leave God out of the equation, have often met with less than stellar success over the long haul.

What's your idea of the "perfect match" between a man and a woman? In the space below, "rapid fire" some words and phrases that come to mind:

_____

_____

_____

_____

_____

In the last few verses of Genesis 2, we can observe six characteristics of the first male-female relationship. As you examine them, think about how these characteristics showcase truths about the relationship between God the Father and Son, and how they also foreshadow the relationship between Christ and the church.

Read Genesis 2:22–25 in the margin. Draw circles and arrows to connect each characteristic to the corresponding phrase. The first one is done for you.

Kinship (my flesh and bones—v. 23)
The man's first realization, upon being presented with his wife, is that they were kin. "Flesh and bones" expresses the notion of family—of individuals connected as part of the same entity, whether by heredity, adoption, or marriage.

Commitment ("hold fast"—v. 24)
The man commits to forsake all others and "hold fast" to his wife. The word means to permanently adhere oneself to. It's the word used of soldering together metal. This joining of husband to wife was a permanent union, orchestrated by God.

Unity ("one"—v. 24)
The word "one" stresses unity while recognizing diversity within that oneness. The same word is used in the famous *shema* of Deuteronomy 6:4: "Hear, O Israel . . . the LORD is One."

Communion ("one flesh"—v. 24)
Husband and wife become "one flesh" through the physical union of their bodies. The act is a physical sign that testifies to their emotional and spiritual union. It's the marital expression of their covenant love, which is grounded in love and is the basis of all true intimacy and communion.

Authenticity ("naked"—v. 25)
Nakedness suggests that the man and woman were at ease with one another without any fear of exploitation or potential for evil. They were authentic, open, and vulnerable, with nothing to hide. They knew each other totally and completely, and were not intimidated or afraid.

Purity ("not ashamed"—v. 25)
We feel shame when we see the chasm between what we are and what we ought to be. For the first man and woman, there was no shame, for there was no sin. Their relationship was pure and holy.

"And the rib that the LORD God had taken from the man he made into a woman and brought her to the man. Then the man said,

'This at last is bone of my bones and flesh of my flesh; she shall be called Woman, because she was taken out of Man.'

Therefore a man shall leave his father and his mother and hold fast to his wife, and they shall become one flesh. And the man and his wife were both naked and were not ashamed."

Genesis 2:22–25

The first male and female experienced what God created the closest of all human relationships to be. Their kinship was perfect. Their commitment was perfect. Their unity was perfect. Their communion was perfect. They were perfectly authentic and pure. Their relationship was paradise!

The chart below describes how the relationship between the first husband and wife showcased truths about the relationships between God the Father and God the Son, and between Christ and His church. Complete the parts of the chart that have been left blank.

Husband ➜ Wife	Father God ➜ Son of God	Christ ➜ Church
Kinship	Jesus is God's only begotten Son. They have a family relationship.	When we believe in Jesus, we are adopted into the family of God
Commit-ment	The Father and Son are committed to each other—God put His covenant "seal" on Christ.	
Unity	Jesus taught that He and the Father are indivisibly "one."	
Communion	Jesus has close "fellowship" with His Father.	
Authenticity	The Father and Son know each other perfectly.	
Purity	Their relationship is pure and holy.	

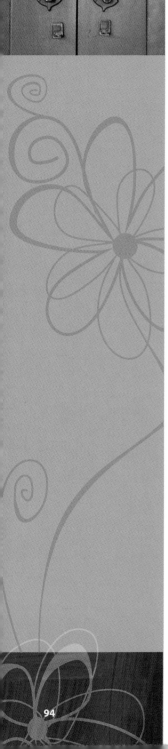

Were you able to complete the chart? The visible relationship between the first husband and wife displayed truths about the invisible relationship between God the Father and His Son. Christ is the only begotten Son of God

(John 3:16). They are indivisible (10:38). God set His covenant "seal" on His Son (6:27). Christ testifies to the fact that He and the Father are one (10:30) and that they experience the intimate communion of perfect love (14:31; 15:9–10). They know each other perfectly (10:15). Their relationship is pure and holy (17:7). Ephesians 5 and numerous other New Testament Scriptures reveal the fact that all of these traits are also characteristic (or should be!) of the relationship between Christ and the church.

Male and female were created in the image of God to put spectacular truths about God on display. The first man and woman showcased these truths flawlessly. Their relationship was amazing. Perfect. Everything a relationship could be! God was pleased. They did a splendid job of putting His glory on display. In God's assessment, the situation was "very good!" (Gen. 1:31). But an observer lurking in the shadows wasn't impressed. There was an enemy in the gate. And it wasn't long before he set about to destroy the magnificent image.

Read 2 Corinthians 4:4 in the margin. Why would Satan ("the god of this world") want to blind people from seeing a truth such as God's design for male and female?

Satan didn't like what the first male-female relationship displayed. At the time, he probably didn't understand that it foreshadowed Christ's relationship to His church-bride. But he could clearly see that this union showcased God's glory. And that irked him, as he hated God and was His sworn enemy! So he determined to destroy this relationship that was designed to reveal the gospel and glory of God.

Because of sin, it's impossible for us to experience the same kind of intimacy that Adam and Eve enjoyed in the garden. But thankfully, we can enjoy the eternal relationship to which a God-glorifying marriage points. Christ makes it possible for us to experience an intimate relationship with God. And when all is said and done, that's what manhood, womanhood, and marriage are intended to reflect.

Why do you think Satan is eager to destroy the kinship, commitment, unity, communion, authenticity, and purity of male-female relationships?

_____

_____

What one practical step can you take to guard against Satan's attempts to destroy these aspects of your marriage and/or other family relationship?

_____

_____

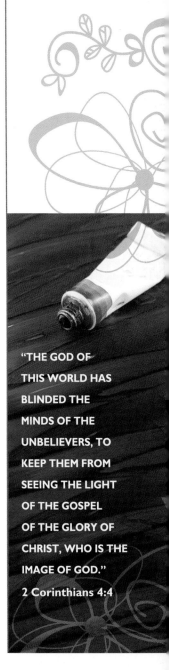

"THE GOD OF THIS WORLD HAS BLINDED THE MINDS OF THE UNBELIEVERS, TO KEEP THEM FROM SEEING THE LIGHT OF THE GOSPEL OF THE GLORY OF CHRIST, WHO IS THE IMAGE OF GOD."

2 Corinthians 4:4

the sales pitch

*H*ave you ever been swayed by a high pressure sales pitch? I'll never forget the time I (Mary) almost bought a superdeluxe-ergonomic-ultrasuction-ultraquiet-hepa-turbo-tornado-vacuum. I was a young mom at home with my first baby when the salesman came calling. It wasn't long before he had me convinced that only his vacuum could save my baby from certain disease and probable death from the masses of microorganisms lurking in my carpet.

To demonstrate its power, he scattered and vacuumed up a handful of metal bullet casings. Wow! If his vacuum could do that, it would surely suck up all those wicked bugs! Only the arrival of my husband saved me from succumbing to what I now chalk up to a hormone-induced gullible state of mind. Brent told the salesman that since we weren't in the habit of leaving metal bullet casings on the carpet, we really didn't need his vacuum.

We laugh about it now, but back then, I was quite taken in by the persuasive sales pitch. You've probably experienced the force of high pressure sales too. I think we all can empathize with the predicament of the first woman in the garden, who was swayed by the subtle deceit of the most effective sales pitch of all time.

Read Satan's sales pitch in your Bible in Genesis 3:1–6. In verse 1, what's the first thing you learn about the Serpent?

_____

_____

Complete the following chart, indicating what this crafty enemy of God said to pitch each idea:

Satan's sales pitch	The words he used to pitch this idea:
God's ways are too restrictive (v. 1).	
You won't suffer consequences (v. 4).	
You'll experience amazing benefits (v. 5).	

 Satan was incredibly crafty and subtle. He knew exactly what to say to push the woman's thoughts in the direction he wanted them to go. He didn't come right out and say that God's ways were too restrictive, that she wouldn't suffer any consequences by going against the Lord, or that she should focus on her own self-interests. He may have assumed that a direct approach wouldn't work. So he craftily introduced subtle lies and distortions. He twisted the truth ever-so-slightly. Once the woman listened to and began to dwell on his false ideas, they contaminated her thinking and enticed her to buy in.

Put an "X" beside the factor that likely did **not** contribute to Eve buying into Satan's sales pitch:

- ☐ She began to dwell on her own right to choose.
- ☐ She began to doubt the goodness of God.
- ☐ She began to doubt the wisdom of God.
- ☐ She began to think that she knew better.
- ☐ She began to question God's motives.
- ☐ She began to claim her independence.

Over and over again, the Scripture teaches that God's laws are for our good and our protection and that obedience brings blessing. But Satan places in our minds the idea that God's laws are burdensome, unreasonable, and unfair, and that if we obey Him, we will be miserable. He tempts us to question God's wisdom.

In that entire, vast garden, God had posted only one Keep Off sign. But Satan caused Eve to focus on that small limitation. He convinced her that by putting restrictions on her behavior, God was depriving her of pleasure and of what was good. Besides doubting His wisdom, she also began to doubt His goodness. Did God really have her best interests at heart? Was He selfishly holding back?

Once we doubt the goodness of God, we feel justified in rejecting His will and making our own decisions about right and wrong. We begin to think that we know better. We begin to claim independence from Him and from the godly counsel He has put in our lives. The truth is that God is good. He is good whether or not we feel or believe He is good. It's not up to us to cast judgment on the goodness of His Word or His ways.

Can you think of a "Keep Off" ("I'm not allowing you to have this") sign that has led you to question God's wisdom and goodness? Explain.

_____

_____

Satan's promise to Eve was tantalizing: "Your eyes will be opened, and you will be like God, knowing good and evil" (Gen. 3:5). Who could resist such an amazing offer?

Eve listened to Satan and mulled over what he told her. According to Genesis 3:6 in the margin, what three things about the forbidden tree made it alluring to her?

1. _____

2. _____

3. _____

> *"So when the woman saw that the tree was good for food, and that it was a delight to the eyes, and that the tree was to be desired to make one wise, she took of its fruit and ate ..."*
>
> **Genesis 3:6**

Eve decided that she could judge the merits of the fruit for herself. First, she decided that it was "*good for food.*" In other words, it appeared edible and tasty. She convinced herself that it wasn't dangerous and wouldn't hurt her. ("It's harmless!") It was also alluring—a "*delight to the eyes.*" ("It looks attractive!") Something so beautiful couldn't possibly be wrong. It held such promise! It was "*desired to make one wise.*" ("It looks

promising!") She was confident that eating it would benefit her greatly.

If the fruit hadn't seemed so appealing, do you think Eve would have fallen for the offer? If it had been rotten and crawling with worms, do you think she would have considered disobeying God? Of course not. What makes Satan's offers so alluring and so deceptive is that they look so right. The Devil is in the business of making sin look harmless, attractive, and promising.

The problem is that Eve didn't stop to evaluate what was really happening. She didn't take the time to discern truth from error. She didn't stop to consider the cost and the consequences of what she was about to do. If Eve

could have imagined the ugly, painful, deadly consequences of her choice—in her own life, in her relationship with God, in her marriage, in her children, in her children's children, and (through the sin of her husband, who followed her) in every human being who would ever live on the planet—do you think she would have listened to Satan's lie and disobeyed God? Probably not.

Describe a situation or circumstance where you were tempted to view sin as harmless, attractive, and promising:

_____

_____

What are some of the consequences we experience in our relationship with God and others when we buy in to Satan's lies and go for his offers?

_____

_____

When Jesus lived on this earth as a man, He experienced what it was to be tempted by Satan. In fact, He was tempted in all the same ways we are (Heb 4:15). But He never once yielded to temptation. By the power of the Spirit and in dependence on God's Word, He overcame the Enemy's lies. Then He died to pay the penalty for our disobedience. Now, by His power within us, we too can be victorious over every scheme and deception of the Evil One.

I'll do it my way!

Have you ever heard that old Frank Sinatra song, "I did it my way"? The lyrics tell the story of a man who is nearing death. As he reflects on his life, he has no regrets for how he lived, saying that, until the end, he did things his way.

There's a cute cartoon that mocks the concept. It features a man, hammer in hand, walking away from several shelves he has just hung on the wall. His T-shirt proudly proclaims the song's theme, "I did it my way!" The look on his face is smug. But it's obvious from the state of the shelves that doing it his way was a horrible mistake.

The shelves are a mess. They're attached to the wall carelessly with too few nails, several of which are bent. The shelves hang at such crooked, ridiculous angles that they're useless. In fact, they're downright dangerous. There's no way they could ever serve any useful purpose. Sure, he did it his way . . . but it's obvious that things would have worked out a whole lot better if he had followed the directions.

The main idea the Serpent pitched to Eve was that she should do things her way. She didn't need God's input. She had the capacity to make good decisions without His help. She could be the judge. The thought he subtly introduced was, *"You have the right. You have the power. You have the potential. You can figure things out yourself. You don't need anyone telling you what to do!"*

Each of Eve's faulty beliefs can be traced back to Satan's sales pitch and the lies he enticed her to believe. The following chart illustrates how the Serpent convinced Eve to do things her own way:

"And Adam was not deceived, but the woman was deceived and became a transgressor."

1 Timothy 2:14

"But I am afraid that as the serpent deceived Eve by his cunning, your thoughts will be led astray from a sincere and pure devotion to Christ."

2 Corinthians 11:3

The Sales Pitch	Judge for YOURSELF . . .	The Buy-In
God's ways are too restrictive.	You have the right ➤	It looks attractive.
You won't suffer consequences.	You have the power ➤	It looks harmless.
You'll experience amazing benefits.	You have the potential ➤	It looks promising.

Examine the chart. What do you think Eve found—and what do people in general find—so compelling about Satan's argument?

_____

_____

The Devil seduced Eve by convincing her that she would receive all kinds of benefits if she would just do it her way. He promised that a whole world of knowledge and experience would open up to her ("Your eyes will be opened"). He assured her that she would be equal with God—that is, she could be her own god ("You will be like God").

Finally, he promised that she would be able to decide for herself what was right and wrong ("knowing good and evil"). God had already told Adam and Eve what was right and what was wrong. But Satan said, in essence, "That's his opinion; you're entitled to your own opinion—you can make your own decisions about what is right and wrong."

Read the verses in the margin of the previous page. Given what you know about the first man and woman, why do you think Satan may have made his pitch to Eve instead of Adam?

_____

_____

Perhaps Satan approached the woman because he thought she would be more likely to respond. Perhaps it was because he knew she would be more vulnerable if he could get her to act independently of her husband. The Bible doesn't tell us why he approached her rather than Adam. But we do know that his approach to the woman deliberately subverted God's design of Adam's headship in the relationship. And we know that Eve was deceived, whereas Adam sinned intentionally and knowingly.

Eve took the bite. But instead of the promised benefits, she found herself with a mouthful of distasteful consequences—guilt, fear, and alienation. The fellowship she had enjoyed with God and her husband was broken. Paradise had been lost.

Read Genesis 3:7–8 in the margin. What did Eve and Adam do after they sinned? Explain why you think they did this.

Imagine the sheer force of awareness and emotion that flooded the woman's spirit when innocence was destroyed. It must have been mind-boggling. The shame. The fear. The overwhelming sense of grief and loss. The cold chill of evil wrapping its black, ugly tentacles around her heart. For the first time ever, she felt embarrassed. Damaged. Unsafe. Exposed. And Adam felt it too. No wonder they sewed fig leaves together in a pitiful effort to cover themselves up.

Along with the guilt and shame, the couple must have experienced other conflicting emotions. They had been infected with sin. So sin immediately took control. Sewing themselves leafy aprons was more than just an attempt to alleviate their shame. It reflected a sense of self-reliance, self-justification, and self-determination. It was another expression of the "I'll do it my way" attitude that had gotten them into trouble in the first place.

Adam and Eve felt they could correct the problem they had just created by coming up with their *own* solution—fig leaves! They didn't need God's help or direction to fix things. They could handle this on their own. So when God came to the garden that evening, they didn't run toward Him. Quite the opposite, in fact. They ran away from God and tried to hide from Him.

What are some ways people try to "cover" up their shame and guilt when they have sinned?

Until that point, Adam and Eve had only known God to be loving, kind, and good. Now they were afraid of Him, hiding from Him. What had happened? Had God changed? No. But they had. Sin had changed them. It had affected their view of who He was and who they were in relation to Him.

Their new mode of thinking was tainted by the sinful premise that God didn't really deserve to be

God. He wasn't smart enough or good enough. He didn't really have their best interests at heart. They had the right to make their own decisions. They deserved to be their own god.

The man and woman hid because they didn't want God to exercise His rightful prerogative as their Creator. They didn't want Him to judge sin or tell them what to do. They wanted to manage and control things on their own. Even when it became clear that they had hopelessly messed things up and couldn't possibly set them straight, they hung on to the deluded belief that they could somehow make their lives work without God.

And since that fateful day, "I'll do it my way" has been the prideful inclination of every man and woman who has ever lived. We mess up our lives by refusing to accept God's boundaries. We mess them up more by trying to cover the resulting problem with our own flimsy, ridiculous efforts. Instead of humbly submitting to God, we stubbornly refuse to believe that He knows better. We are literally "hell-bent" to do it our own way.

Put an "X" on the scale to indicate how often you feel the "I'll do it my way" attitude crop up in your heart.

Seldom   Often

Can you identify an instance or time (past or present) in your life in which your attitude has been "I'll do it my way," and you have resisted God's way? What do such attitudes and choices reveal about your heart, and what consequences have you experienced?

_____

_____

How do Christ's perfect obedience to His Father and His death on the cross spell hope for those who have bought into Satan's lies?

_____

_____

"Then the eyes of both of them were opened, and they realized they were naked; so they sewed fig leaves together and made coverings for themselves. Then the man and his wife heard the sound of the LORD God as he was walking in the garden in the cool of the day, and they hid from the LORD God among the trees of the garden. But the LORD God called to the man, "Where are you?" He answered, "I heard you in the garden, and I was afraid because I was naked; so I hid."

Genesis 3: 7–10 NIV

Generally speaking, we don't fall into bondage overnight. We don't just wake up one morning and discover that we're addicted to food, or have a temper we can't control, or are seething with criticism and rebellion in a marriage. In my (Nancy's) book *Lies Women Believe*, I trace the progression of how deception leads to bondage. There's a progression that usually begins with listening to a lie.

That's how it all began in the garden of Eden. Eve listened to the lies told her by Satan. I'm confident she had no idea where those lies would ultimately lead her and her family. Perhaps it didn't seem particularly dangerous just to listen to the Serpent—to hear him out, to see what he had to say. Listening in itself wasn't disobedience. But—and here's the key—listening to a viewpoint that was contrary to God's Word put Eve on a slippery slope that led to disobedience, conflict in her relationships, and spiritual death.

Listening to counsel or ways of thinking that are not according to the Truth is the first step in a downward spiral into bondage. First we listen to a lie; then we dwell on it. We begin to consider what the Enemy has said. We mull it over in our minds. It's as though we engage in conversation with him, as Eve did. At this point, the seed that has been sown takes root and starts to grow.

Eve listened to the Serpent's sales pitch. Then she considered it and engaged him in further discussion. Before long, she believed that what he told her was true—even though it clearly contradicted God. Once she believed the lie, the final step was a small one.

Listen to the lie, dwell on it, believe it, and sooner or later you'll act on it. Act on a lie repeatedly, and you will find yourself on a path to bondage.

| Listen | → | Dwell | → | Believe | → | Act |

Most of us mindlessly accept whatever we hear and see. We listen to music, read books and magazines, watch TV programs, go to movies, surf the Internet, listen to advice, and respond to advertisements. We adopt the latest fads, and embrace the lifestyles, values, and priorities of our friends.

We listen to what the world has to say about womanhood and how we should dress, act, think, and behave. We do all this without asking ourselves important questions: What is the message here? Is it really true? Am I being deceived by a way of thinking that is contrary to the Truth?

Try to identify some subtle lies about womanhood that Satan has pitched to you. Have you progressed from listening to believing to acting on any of these lies?

_____

_____

If you do things your way instead of God's way, you'll invariably find that things don't work out the way you thought they would. You may get a bite of the "apple" you wanted, but sooner or later, the fruit will turn sour in your mouth.

Read Genesis 3:7–10 on the previous page. Satan promised that Eve's eyes would be opened. But what were they opened to? Check all the things she likely saw:

- [ ] She saw that she was naked.
- [ ] She saw that she had been infected with evil.
- [ ] She saw that she was guilty.
- [ ] She saw that she was no longer pure.
- [ ] She saw that she had been unfaithful.
- [ ] She saw that her relationships were damaged.
- [ ] She saw that she had rejected God.
- [ ] She saw that she deserved condemnation.
- [ ] She saw that her choice could never be undone.
- [ ] She saw that life would soon return to normal.
- [ ] She saw that she had destroyed paradise.

Can you think of anything else her eyes may have been opened to?

_____

_____

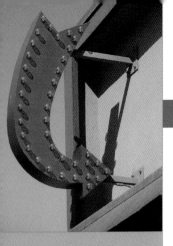

not my fault

But the LORD God called to the man, "Where are you?" He answered, "I heard you in the garden, and I was afraid because I was naked; so I hid." And he said, "Who told you that you were naked? Have you eaten from the tree that I commanded you not to eat from?" The man said, "The woman you put here with me—she gave me some fruit from the tree, and I ate it." Then the LORD God said to the woman, "What is this you have done?" The woman said, "The serpent deceived me, and I ate."

Genesis 3: 9–13 NIV

After Adam and Eve ate the forbidden fruit, God called them out to hold them accountable for what they had done. Notice that God did not approach them as a family unit. He didn't ask, "What have you [plural] done?" Neither did He ask Adam and Eve to explain each other's behavior. He didn't ask Adam, "What did Eve do?"—nor did He ask Eve, "What did your husband do?" He approached Adam first, then Eve, and asked each one individually, "What have you [singular] done?"

Read Genesis 3:9–13 in the margin. Do you think Adam and Eve were truly sorry for their sin? Explain why or why not.

_____

_____

Put an "A" beside the response that you think best reflects Adam's and Eve's attitude. Put a "B" beside the response that best reflects an attitude of repentance.

_____ I'm sorry your feelings were hurt.
_____ I'm sorry, it wasn't my fault.
_____ I'm sorry I got caught.
_____ I'm sorry, I was very wrong.

God was looking for a simple admission of guilt. He wanted them to "*fess up.*" But as the account unfolds, we see that Adam and Eve both chose to play "The Blame Game" rather than take personal responsibility for their actions. Adam blamed the woman, and the woman blamed the Serpent.

In both cases, their response was technically correct. Eve *was* the woman God had given to Adam. And she *had* given the fruit to her husband. The Serpent *had*, in fact, deceived Eve. However, by shifting the blame to another, Adam and Eve were trying to diminish their own responsibility in the matter.

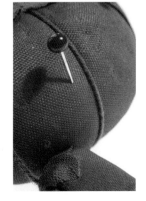

God didn't ask them what someone else had done to make them sin; He held them accountable for their own behavior. Regardless of what had influenced them to make that choice, it was still their choice.

Adam and Eve may have been the first, but they certainly weren't the last in what has become a long, unbroken line of "blame-shifters." When we are angry, depressed, bitter, annoyed, impatient, or fearful, our natural response is to shift at least some of the responsibility onto the people or circumstances that we think "made" us that way.

We have both heard countless women trying to explain the circumstances that "caused" their indebtedness, their eating disorder, their immorality, their marriage breakdown, or a strained relationship.

Only seldom do we hear a woman take personal responsibility for her choices that have contributed to the issues in her life. God is "calling you out" to take responsibility instead of blaming others. Through humility, and with the help of the Holy Spirit, you can counteract your natural tendency to play the blame game.

Describe a time in recent weeks that you failed to take responsibility, and instead blamed circumstances or other people for your bad attitude or behavior.

_____

_____

Take a moment to "fess up" in prayer. Ask the Lord to help you take personal responsibility for your choices, to acknowledge where you have chosen your way rather than His.

_____

_____

The women's movement in our day has been characterized by a tendency to blame men and point out their sin, while absolving women of any personal responsibility. Pointing a finger at others keeps us in guilt and bondage. Freedom comes from taking responsibility for our choices —the things we listen to, thoughts we dwell on, how we choose to respond— and from looking to Christ for forgiveness, mercy, and grace.

me vs. we

The Lord hadn't even yet explained the consequences of sin, and cracks were already showing up in Adam and Eve's relationship. When questioned, Adam shirked his responsibility, shifted the blame, and sharply accused his wife.

How would you feel if someone you loved and trusted and had a wonderful relationship with suddenly turned on you? For Eve, the pain and shock must have been unspeakable. Adam—her soul mate—had never spoken a harsh or critical word. He had loved her, protected her, and delighted in her. They were perfect together. They were united as one. But all that changed in an instant. She must have been blindsided by her husband's Jekyll-and-Hyde-type transformation.

Adam's words cut deep. They implied that God had made a mistake in fashioning *her* as his wife—that he would have been better off without a woman. At that moment, did a crusty layer of self-protection form around her heart? Did she take an ever-so-slight step away from his side? Did she wrap her arms around herself and hold the leaves tighter to her chest?

He was being ugly. It wasn't her fault. She'd been terribly deceived. The Serpent had tricked her. Why hadn't Adam done something? Why hadn't he intervened? He was standing right there! Didn't he understand? Didn't he care? She'd had the wool pulled over her eyes. He hadn't. He'd neglected his responsibility. And yet he had the gall to turn on her and blame her for his own willful disobedience! To save his own skin, Adam, her wonderful protector, was tossing her to the wolves.

Can you think of a time when someone you thought was on your side turned on you? Describe how you felt.

_____

_____

Broken communion between God and man immediately resulted in broken communion between man and woman. Their unity was severely damaged. It was no longer, "We're in this together!" Instead, sin poisoned them with the attitude, "Every man for himself!" and "Every woman for herself!"

losing sight of we

The first relationship mirrored the image of God. In the Trinity, individual and distinct beings are joined in an inseparable unity. The individual members (Father, Son, and Spirit) are joined as part of the collective whole (God). In their relationship the "me" is not the focus as much as the "we."

Before they sinned, the first couple's relationship reflected this pattern. They had healthy self-identities and a healthy interdependence. The "we" they experienced with God enabled them to enjoy an attitude of "we" with one another. But sin destroyed all this. Once they claimed independence from God and focused on the "me," they lost sight of themselves as "we." As a result, they began to point fingers and play the blame game.

Sin caused humans to become preoccupied with *self*. Our focus became "*MY* way!" "*ME* first!" "*MY* needs." Or "I need you to define *ME*!" The shift was dramatic. And it immediately resulted in a strain on the male-female relationship, leading to an "us versus them" mentality.

What are some ways in which an "us versus them" mind-set shows up between male and female in contemporary culture?

Read 1 Corinthians 11:11–12 on page 110. Which word best describes a godly view of man and woman?

- ☐ independent
- ☐ competing
- ☐ clinging
- ☐ separate
- ☐ interconnected

To be *independent* means that you see yourself as separate and distinct; that you act apart from and without regard to; that you refuse to let your behavior be affected or influenced by; that you are free from the support or help of; that you do not need, want, or accept what the other has to offer.

Interdependence is a healthy, reciprocal relationship in which parties are mutually influenced by, supported by, and helped by one another. They are interconnected. They trust and rely on each other's unique contribution. That's what God intended for the male-female relationship.

It's important to note that interdependence differs from what is sometimes called "codependence"—that is, an unhealthy relationship in which an individual's sense of identity and worth is wrapped up in the other person.

What are some examples of the way culture encourages women to assert their independence from men?

_____

_____

How do you think a woman's behavior might change if she had a stronger sense of "we" in her marriage?

_____

_____

> *"In the Lord woman is not independent of man nor man of woman; for as woman was made from man, so man is now born of woman. And all things are from God."*
>
> **I Corinthians 11:11–12**

> *"If one member suffers, all suffer together; if one member is honored, all rejoice together. Now you are the body of Christ and individually members of it."*
>
> **I Corinthians 12:26–27**

A friend once reminded me, "Mary, if you insult your husband, you insult yourself, if you wound him, you wound yourself, if you benefit him, you benefit yourself—whatever you do to him, you do to you." That wise counsel brings to mind Proverbs 14:1: "The wisest of women builds her house, but folly with her own hands tears it down."

God created the human race to be united. But sin pitted men against women—not just in the marriage relationship but in society as a whole. When it comes to female and male, we often have an "us" versus "them" mentality. Women ridicule and belittle men. Men objectify and demean women. We argue about who is better. We compete. We point fingers and blame. We forget that we're connected—that we're in this together.

How would you describe your attitude toward men? Do you tend to be more independent or interdependent? Explain.

_____

_____

Do you think your attitude is in line with God's ideal? If not, how could you bring it more in line?

_____

_____

The Lord does not want woman to function independent of man. Nor does He want woman to be unhealthily dependent on man, looking to him to meet all her needs. He wants male and female to be interdependent on one another—to value each other, and be mutually influenced, supported, and helped by one another. The Lord wants the marriage relationship—and the relationship between males and females in general —to showcase the kinship, commitment, unity, communion, authenticity, and purity that are the hallmark of His relationships.

This week, we've seen how the Serpent set about to destroy the image that God designed for male and female to display. Have you noticed that Satan's tactics really haven't changed? He tempts us to fall for the idea that our lives will be better when we take matters into our own hands and decide for ourselves how we want to live. He tries to get us to leave God out of the equation and to focus on our rights, our power, and our potential. He wants us to have a "do it myself," independent spirit that plays the blame game, and sets men up as the enemy; or a needy spirit that sets men up as god, and turns to them to fill the relational vacuum in our hearts.

→ **Next week** we'll take a look at some further consequences of the fall on male-female relationships. It's more bad news. But in the midst of tragedy came the amazing promise that the horrible consequences of sin would one day be overcome by One who would crush the Serpent's head.

"THE BODY IS ONE AND HAS MANY MEMBERS, AND ALL THE MEMBERS OF THE BODY, THOUGH MANY, ARE ONE BODY . . . ."
1 Corinthians 12:12

"FOR AS IN ONE BODY WE HAVE MANY MEMBERS, AND THE MEMBERS DO NOT ALL HAVE THE SAME FUNCTION, SO WE, THOUGH MANY, ARE ONE BODY IN CHRIST, AND INDIVIDUALLY MEMBERS ONE OF ANOTHER."
Romans 12:4–5

drawing it out, drawing it in...

snake in my garden

process

The video for Week Four will help you process this week's lessons. You'll find this week's video, a downloadable outline, and many more resources at www.TrueWoman101.com/week4.

ponder

Think about the following questions. Discuss them with your friends, family, and/or small group:

1. Refer to the characteristics of Adam and Eve's relationship outlined on page 94. Which characteristic do you find the most appealing? Why?

2. In what way did the first male-female relationship put God on display? Why do you think Satan wanted to destroy God's design?

3. What do you think Eve found compelling about Satan's sales pitch? (See page 96.) Describe a situation where you were tempted to view sin as harmless, attractive, and promising.

4. What's the problem with having an "I'll do it my way" attitude? What ideas about God does this type of attitude reveal?

5. Identify some subtle lies about womanhood that Satan commonly pitches to women. Are you guilty of listening, dwelling, believing, and/or acting on any of these lies? Do you blame circumstances or people for your poor choices? Do you blame men?

6. What's the difference between independence and interdependence? Why does culture encourage woman to assert her independence from man? How does this impact male-female relationships?

7. Have you ever fallen for Satan's sales pitch? Describe how there is/has been a "snake in your garden" with regard to your womanhood.

personalize

Use the following lined page to journal. Write down what you learned this week. Record your comments, a favorite verse, or a concept or quote that was particularly helpful or meaningful to you. Compose a prayer, letter, or poem. Jot down notes from the video or your small group session. Express your heart response to what you have studied. Personalize this week's lessons in the way that will best help you apply them to your life.

personalize it

drawing it out,
drawing it in . . .

battle of the sexes

One of the most talked about events in U.S. sports history was the 1973 tennis match between Billie Jean King and Bobby Riggs. Over 30,000 enthusiasts packed the Houston Astrodome, and more than 50 million viewers from around the world watched the event on television. Legendary sportscaster Howard Cosell provided commentary.

Billie Jean King made her entrance to the blaring refrain "Anything you can do, I can do better!" She came in Cleopatra-style, aloft on a red velvet litter carried by four bare-chested musclemen dressed in the garb of ancient slaves.

Her male opponent, Bobby Riggs, followed in a rickshaw drawn by a bevy of scantily-clad, well-endowed playboy-type models. The highly touted "Battle of the Sexes" was set to begin.

The feminist movement was at its height. Title IX had just passed, and twenty-nine-year-old Billie Jean King was a vocal proponent of sexual equality in sports. This six-time Wimbledon singles/four-time U.S. Open champion had started a women's sports magazine and a women's sports foundation, and had aggressively petitioned for female professional athletes to be paid the same as male athletes. King was the star of the new Virginia Slims Tennis Tour, and the poster child for their mantra, "You've Come a Long Way, Baby!"

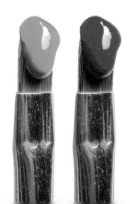

Bobby Riggs, age fifty-five, was a former Wimbledon champion. In his heyday, he was one of the best, but in a sport where thirty-five is considered over the hill, Riggs was downright ancient. Though he hadn't competed professionally in decades, Riggs was a notorious hustler who used tennis exhibitions to gamble revenue. He placed wages on himself with gimmicks, such as using a frying pan instead of a tennis racquet and typically finished with a profit.

Riggs noticed the publicity being generated from the women's liberation movement. He set about to capitalize on the media attention by making outlandish sexist comments about the superiority of men over women. He described himself as a "chauvinist pig" and even said that he wanted to be the number one pig. Riggs boasted that even an old man such as himself could defeat a woman in her prime. Male athletes were simply better—no matter what their age.

Riggs had already soundly defeated Australian tennis champion Margaret Court, the top-ranked women's player in the world, in a match referred to as the "Mother's Day Massacre." His victory placed him on the cover of *Sports Illustrated* and *Time* magazine. In order to salvage the respect of women's tennis, which had suffered greatly from Court's defeat to a fifty-five-year-old has-been, King agreed to play Riggs in this ultimate, deciding "Battle of the Sexes" showdown.

She trounced him in three straight sets.

An entire generation of Americans would remember the "Battle of the Sexes" the way they would remember a spectacular Super Bowl or a great World Series. Women had come a long, long way. It was a new era. King had shut up the condescending Riggs and other chauvinist pigs like him, and proved once and for all that women were the superior sex.

Few women of today's generation remember the match between Billie Jean King and Bobby Riggs. When they hear the idiom the "Battle of the Sexes," they're more likely to think about a reality TV show or the modern-day board game "The Battle of the Sexes: The Battle Continues."

The subtitle of the board game got it right. The battle does continue. It wasn't settled by King and Riggs. Women and men still vie to prove who is better. And the battle didn't start with the 1973 tennis match either. As you'll soon see, it's almost as old as time. This week, you'll learn that this particular battle isn't just the stuff of jokes, entertainment, media gimmicks, and lighthearted party banter. It's a painfully real consequence of sin that wreaks havoc in male-female relationships. It's alarming, serious stuff. No man or woman on the face of this earth is unaffected by the primordial battle of the sexes that came about as a result of the fall. →

united we fall

"[God] said, 'Who told you that you were naked? Have you eaten of the tree of which I commanded you not to eat?' The man said, 'The woman whom you gave to be with me, she gave me fruit of the tree, and I ate.' Then the LORD God said to the woman, 'What is this that you have done?' The woman said, 'The serpent deceived me, and I ate.'"

Genesis 3:11–13

Last week we left off our study of Genesis at the point where God was confronting Adam and Eve about their sin. When God asked Adam about eating the forbidden fruit, Adam immediately blamed Eve. Eve, in turn, blamed the Serpent for tricking her. The woman *had* been tricked. Paul confirms that the Serpent "deceived Eve by his cunning" (2 Cor. 11:3). But he notes this didn't let her off the hook. She still became a sinner (1 Tim. 2:14). By the same token, the fact that Eve took the first bite didn't let Adam off the hook. Adam was guilty. He personally "transgressed the covenant" (Hos. 6:7).

God held Adam and Eve accountable. Adam was held accountable for his sin, and Eve was held accountable for hers. God knew that Eve sinned first and Adam second. He knew that Eve was deceived, and Adam was not. He knew that the factors and motivators that led them to sin were different.

But although Adam and Eve sinned at different times and in different ways, God determined that "all" had sinned and fallen short of His glory. And this would be the case throughout the rest of human history (Rom. 3:23). Man and woman were in the same boat. When they indulged in the forbidden fruit, the whole human race fell.

Adam was the firstborn. He was the representative head of the human race. Adam was accountable for the well-being of the human family, so God held him ultimately responsible. "In *Adam* all die" (1 Cor. 15:22). The first Adam points to another "Adam" (v. 45) who would die as humanity's representative and reverse the tragic consequences of sin, as the apostle Paul points out in Romans 5:

> *[Adam] was a type of the one who was to come. But the free gift is not like the trespass* (Rom. 5:14–15).

Therefore, as one trespass led to condemnation for all men, so one act of righteousness leads to justification and life for all men. For as by the one man's disobedience the many were made sinners, so by the one man's obedience the many will be made righteous (Rom. 5:18–19).

Where sin increased, grace abounded all the more, so that, as sin reigned in death, grace also might reign through righteousness leading to eternal life through Jesus Christ our Lord. (Rom. 5:20–21)

On the following chart, use phrases from the passage above to compare and contrast the first Adam to Jesus (the "last Adam"). The first point is recorded for you:

First Adam (Man's Sin)	Last Adam (God's Gift)
Led to condemnation	Led to justification

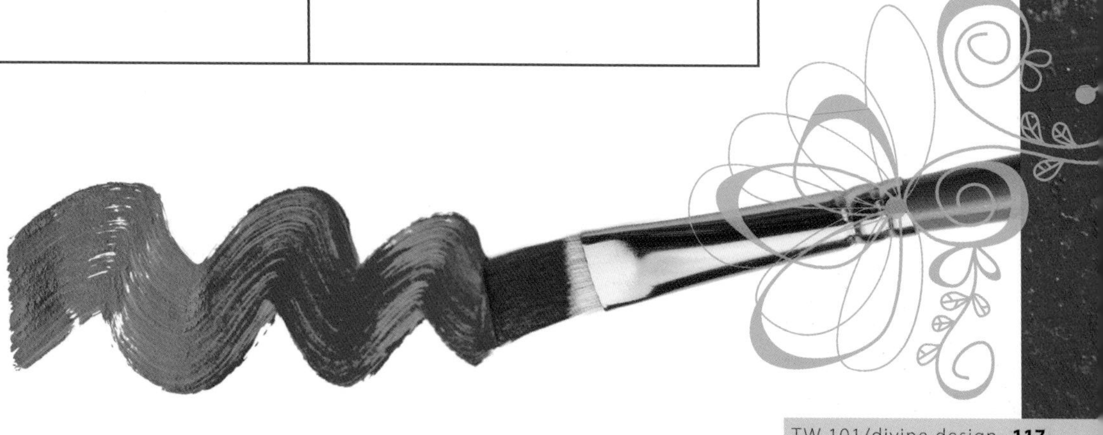

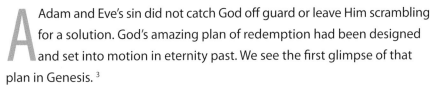

glimmer of hope

Adam and Eve's sin did not catch God off guard or leave Him scrambling for a solution. God's amazing plan of redemption had been designed and set into motion in eternity past. We see the first glimpse of that plan in Genesis. [3]

After giving Adam and Eve a chance to explain their behavior, God cursed the Serpent. He didn't bother to ask the Serpent to explain what he had done, He merely pronounced the punishment. Theologians call Genesis 3:14–15 the "*protoevangelion*"—the first telling of the gospel—because it's the first place in the Bible that anticipates the good news of the coming Savior.

Read Genesis 3:14–15 in the margin. Imagine you are Eve. What would you have thought and felt about God's judgment on the Serpent? Why?

_____

_____

Eve must have listened intently to the curse the Lord placed on the one who had crafted her downfall. First, the Serpent that had appeared so attractive and winsome would forever crawl on his belly and eat dirt. The image is one of extreme humiliation.

Second, there would be "enmity" between the woman and the Serpent and between their offspring. This doesn't mean that women would hate snakes (though most of us do!). "Enmity" describes a murderous level of animosity and the type of intense hostility expressed in war (Num. 35:21; Ezek. 25:15). It indicates a fierce conflict of life-and-death proportions.

Finally, God foretold: "He shall bruise your head, and you shall bruise his heel." This speaks of the battle between Christ and Satan. God knew that the two would fight and wound each other. But Christ's wound would heal (and would become a means of sinners being healed), whereas Satan's wound would be fatal. Jesus would ultimately crush Satan under his feet (Rom. 16:20). In essence, God told Satan:

> "Eat dirt!"
> "The fight is on!"
> "You're going to lose!!"

Eve couldn't have fully understood what God was talking about, but she must have caught the glimmer of hope. God's promise that the seed of the woman would be victorious over the Serpent confirmed that His great love, grace, and mercy would triumph over Satan, sin, and judgment.

"The Lord God said to the serpent, 'Because you have done this, cursed are you above all livestock and above all beasts of the field; on your belly you shall go, and dust you shall eat all the days of your life. I will put enmity between you and the woman, and between your offspring and her offspring; he shall bruise your head, and you shall bruise his heel.'"

Genesis 3:14–15

Just imagine how Eve must have felt at that moment. She probably hadn't yet fully processed the conflicting emotions of disgust and fascination that rushed in when her eyes were opened to sin. She was likely still reeling from the flood of hurt, resentment, and self-protective blame that swept over her with Adam's betrayal. Not only that, she had to deal with the shame and self-consciousness of standing in God's holy presence. She probably couldn't look Him in the eye.

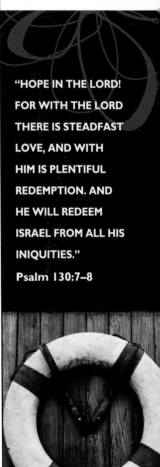

What's more, she was likely terrified about the prospect of His judgment. Since she had swallowed the Serpent's lie that God didn't have her best interests at heart, she was afraid about how He would let the hammer fall. Perhaps Eve trembled violently with the force of her overwhelming emotions. If you were in her position, wouldn't you?

The Lord may have judged the Serpent first because He wanted to reassure Adam and Eve of His great love, and to give them a glimpse of His marvelous plan. He wanted to give them hope.

Read Psalm 130:7–8 in the margin. Explain why the psalmist encouraged people to hope in God.

_____

_____

It is amazing that in the garden of Eden the Lord held out hope for the defeat of sin before He even explained its consequences to the man and the woman. What a loving, gracious God He is! In this fallen world, we all experience the brokenness of sin, but God wants us to focus on His hope and deliverance, and to rely on His power to overcome the Serpent and his schemes.

Is there a relationship, sin, or struggle for which you need hope and deliverance? Identify it here:

_____

_____

→ **Over the next few days,** we'll be looking at how the male-female relationship has been damaged by sin, and how the battle of the sexes creates pain and havoc in our lives. But before we do, you need to know that with God there's hope. Through the decisive victory Christ won on the cross, there's always hope! Spend some time praying about the situation you identified above. Ask the Lord for His strength and wisdom. Resolve to hope in God's steadfast love and plentiful redemption.

"HOPE IN THE LORD! FOR WITH THE LORD THERE IS STEADFAST LOVE, AND WITH HIM IS PLENTIFUL REDEMPTION. AND HE WILL REDEEM ISRAEL FROM ALL HIS INIQUITIES."
Psalm 130:7–8

gender bender

A common feature in children's magazines is the "What's wrong with this picture?" game. The child examines a picture or illustration and tries to identify things that are out of place or wrong. A fish in a flowerpot, an upside-down photo, an apple for a doorknob, or a chair with two legs, for example. The game requires a basic level of understanding about the appropriate arrangement and use of things. A child who doesn't know that a fish needs water might not notice anything amiss about a fish in a flowerpot.

In the first few weeks of this study, we examined the basics of God's divine design for male and female. Using that knowledge, we can take a look at the fall and observe a few things wrong with the picture.

The couple is together in the garden. The Serpent approaches them, apparently ignores the man, and strikes up a conversation with the woman, fully aware that God has placed her under the protection and authority of her husband, and that both of them are under God's authority. (Notice Satan's strategy to subvert God's authority structure by going directly to the woman.) Satan starts the exchange by asking her a question: "Did God really say, 'You must not eat from any tree in the garden'?" (Gen. 3:1 NIV)

At this point notice what the woman does *not* do. She does not acknowledge her husband, who is standing by her side. She does not say to the Serpent, "I'd like for you to meet my husband." She does not turn to her husband and say, "Honey, how do you think we should respond?" or "Adam, why don't you tell him what God said to you?" She carries on the entire conversation with the Serpent as if her husband were not there.

Furthermore, when it comes time to make a choice, she takes matters into her own hands. She does not consult with her husband on this important

> "If we all started out in Edenic bliss, why is life so painful now? Genesis 3 explains why. And if something has gone terribly wrong, do we have any hope of restoration? Genesis 3 gives us hope."[1]
>
> **Raymond C. Ortlund Jr.**

matter. She does not ask his input or direction; she simply acts: "She took and ate it" (Gen. 3:6 NIV).

And what is Adam doing this whole time? He is doing what a lot of women tell us their husbands do much of the time: *nothing*. He doesn't interfere; he doesn't get involved—except to passively accept and eat some fruit himself when his wife hands it to him.

Based on the roles and responsibilities God gave Adam and Eve, "What's wrong with this picture?" Explain what you think was amiss in Adam and Eve's behavior (hint: Gen. 3:17 might help):

_____

_____

God created the first human couple to complement each other and work together as one. He gave man the capability and responsibility to initiate—to protect and provide for those under his care; to *lead and feed* them. He created the woman to respond to the initiative of her husband. She was to function in relationship to him—not independent of him. They were each created with a

unique design so they could come together and operate as a unified whole. Even the obvious physiological differences between men and women express this fundamental truth.

But who is "leading and feeding" in this account? Not the man, but the woman. And who is responding rather than initiating? Not the woman, but the man. And why aren't they relationally collaborating as one? Something is very wrong with this picture. And ever since that fateful day in Eden, God's beautiful created order has been marred and twisted by sin.

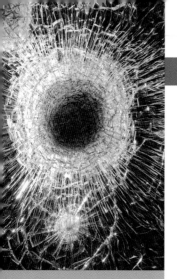

When humanity fell, it came under the sentence of death, which was the ultimate consequence of eating the forbidden fruit (Gen. 3:19). Death is the end of life (physical death). But it is also separation from God (spiritual death). This death sentence affects male and female equally.

But there were also other consequences to sin. After the fall, God pronounced punishment on the man and woman sex-specifically. The woman received a different sentence than the man. The sentences were linked to the way in which the sexes were created, and the way in which they had violated God's divine design. Because men and women were different, they would experience the effects of sin in different ways.

Read Genesis 3:16–17 in the margin. In the space below, summarize the sex-specific consequences of sin:

Women will: _____

_____

_____

Men will: _____

_____

_____

> "To the woman he said, 'I will surely multiply your pain in childbearing; in pain you shall bring forth children. Your desire shall be for your husband, and he shall rule over you.' And to Adam he said, '. . .cursed is the ground because of you; in pain you shall eat of it all the days of your life.'"
>
> **Genesis 3:16–17**

We know that everyone sins and falls short of the glory of God. But have you ever considered the fact that sin affects us sex-specifically? Sin messes with a man's manhood. Sin messes with a woman's womanhood. It messes up who God created us to be as MEN and WOMEN. It bends gender.

God pronounced that the *woman* would experience hardship in being a mother ("pain in childbearing") and a wife ("desire . . . for your husband"). Her **relationships** would suffer. She would have a tough time being a woman. He pronounced that the *man* would experience hardship in providing for and protecting his family. His **capability** (efficacy, power to produce effects) would suffer. He would have a tough time being a man. That which once brought joy and unity would become a source of pain and frustration.

Fill in the blanks to complete the statements (hint: refer to the previous paragraph for help):

Woman is a *relational* being. Sin affects her _____.

Man is an *initiatory* being. Sin affects his _____.

In Genesis 3:16–17 in the margin of the previous page, circle each instance of the word "pain."

"Pain" refers to physical pain as well as emotional sorrow. Closely related Hebrew words indicate that it can involve the following emotions:

- grief
- sadness
- fatigue
- weariness

- irritation
- anger
- bitterness
- despair

- distaste
- disgust
- agitation
- turmoil

Underline each emotion you've personally experienced in relationships.

"Pain" is the tragic consequence of sin for both women and men. Tomorrow, we'll take a closer look at the specifics of what this means for each sex. But suffice it to say for now that men experience the pain of manhood just as much as women experience the pain of womanhood. If you were to ask a guy to put a check beside each emotion he's experienced in his effort to "make things work," he'd probably check off just as many emotions as you did. Women keenly feel the pain in their relationships; men keenly feel it in their capacity to succeed (including their capacity to succeed in relationships).

Sadly, as long as there's sin in this world, men and women will inevitably experience pain and death. Thankfully, Jesus came to take the "sting" out of this punishment (1 Cor. 15:55–56). God's unbelievable promise is that one day, even this consequence will be reversed for those who accept His incredible gift of salvation.

Read Revelation 21:4 in the margin. What are some attitudes and/or behaviors in relationships that induce pain, which you would like to see "pass away"?

_____

_____

→ **Spend some time in prayer,** thanking the Lord that one day all the pain of fallen manhood and womanhood will come to an end.

> "HE WILL WIPE AWAY EVERY TEAR FROM THEIR EYES, AND DEATH SHALL BE NO MORE, NEITHER SHALL THERE BE MOURNING, NOR CRYING, NOR PAIN ANYMORE, FOR THE FORMER THINGS HAVE PASSED AWAY."
> **Revelation 21:4**

right where it hurts

O Over the years, I (Nancy) have discovered that every God-given strength, if not perpetually safeguarded and surrendered to His control, can become an area of weakness and failure. It is precisely in the realm of those strengths that the Enemy often targets us for attack—knowing that if he can bring us down at those points, we will be more likely to concede territory to him in other areas. In that sense, a person's greatest strength may also be their greatest area of vulnerability.

The Serpent was incredibly crafty. There in the garden, he apparently recognized and intentionally targeted the unique design of the man and the woman. He subtly leveraged Eve's beautiful, responsive spirit—while undermining Adam's capability to lead and feed. Satan knew that each gender's respective strength also provided a point of vulnerability. In attacking the essence of Eve's womanhood and Adam's manhood, Satan hit them in the spot where he knew it would do the greatest damage. He hit them right where it would hurt the most.

And hurt it did. Yesterday we learned that "pain" is part of the sex-specific judgment against woman, and also part of the sex-specific judgment against man. Today we want to explore a bit further some of the ramifications of sin in both womanhood and manhood.

> *"To the woman he said, 'I will surely multiply your pain in childbearing; in pain you shall bring forth children. Your desire shall be for your husband, and he shall rule over you.'"*
>
> **Genesis 3:16**

the pain of womanhood

According to yesterday's lesson, what unique aspect of womanhood is damaged by sin?

_____

_____

The first part of woman's sentence in Genesis 3:16 deals with her relationship to her children. God said her pain in "childbearing" and "bringing forth children" would be "multiplied." Because of sin, the whole process of having children became much more difficult than it was supposed to be.

"Bringing forth children" includes all the hormonal and menstrual functions of a woman, as well as pregnancy and the physical act of giving birth. Not all women can attest to the pain of labor and childbirth. But we all experience the ongoing challenges of living in a female body.

However, the physical aspect of bearing children pales in comparison to the emotional, spiritual, and relational dimensions. "Childbearing" involves the whole process of raising and interacting with a child. The pain and difficulty of motherhood is far more than physical.

Eve found that out the hard way when her oldest son grew jealous of his younger brother and murdered him in cold blood. Mothers know what it is to "hurt" for a child. We ache. We worry. We pray. We hope. We lie awake at night. We cry. Being a mother is one of the most satisfying, and because of sin, one of the most painful of all relationships.

Another relationship that is severely affected by sin is a woman's relationship to men—and specifically to her husband.

Fill in the missing words of Genesis 3:16:

"Your _____ shall be _____ your husband,

and he shall rule _____ you."

God created woman's responsiveness and man's headship to be beautiful, unifying elements of the male-female relationship. But sin twists these things into ugly, destructive, competing forces. Woman's "*desire for*" man is twisted in a negative way. And so is man's "*rule over*" woman.

We can get an idea for what this means by comparing it to a verse that uses the same Hebrew words and structure. In Genesis 4:7, God warns Cain: *"Sin is crouching at the door. Its desire is for you, but you must rule over it."* Sin's obsessive desire to stalk and control Cain, and the crushing rule Cain was challenged to exercise over sin, give us a hint as to how the male-female relationship was damaged by the fall. This ugly picture stands in contrast to the beautiful interaction male and female enjoyed before the fall.

Theologians have talked a lot about what this phrase in Genesis 3:16 means, but here's what we think it comes down to. God is saying to the woman: You will have the urge to control, resist, oppose, and act against your husband. Whereas you were intended to function as one—in harmony, in peace, in unity—there

will be a barrier between you. Instead of following your husband's lead and pulling together with him in seeking to serve and glorify God, you'll have the inclination to grab control of the reins and independently go your own way.

The end of that verse says not only will your desire be against your husband, but "he shall rule over you." That suggests that sometimes he will exhibit a rule (headship, oversight, authority) that is self-centered, dictatorial, autocratic, or harsh. He will not always lead in a godly way. In a more general sense, the judgment could be stated like this:

> *Sin twisted the positive desire of **woman** to respond amenably to man into a negative desire to resist and rebel against him.*

> *Sin twisted the positive drive of **man** to use his strength to lead, protect, and provide for woman into a negative tendency to abuse her or to abdicate his responsibility toward her.*

Describe ways in which you have witnessed the painful reality of these male and female sin tendencies:

_____

_____

This is the beginning of the battle of the sexes. God created the sexes to live in oneness and harmony. But sin changed all that. Sin damaged woman's inherent softness. Sin also damaged man's inherent strength. Sin twists and distorts gender and creates pain in the male-female relationship. It pits male and female against each other.

the pain of manhood

W Woman is not the only one who experiences pain. The Lord also sentenced man to pain. Man was created as an initiator. He was to provide for his family and protect them. But because of sin, his efforts were frustrated. The environment over which he

"And to Adam he said, '. . . cursed is the ground because of you; in pain you shall eat of it all the days of your life; thorns and thistles it shall bring forth for you; and you shall eat the plants of the field. By the sweat of your face you shall eat bread, till you return to the ground, for out of it you were taken; for you are dust, and to dust you shall return.'"

Genesis 3:17–19

was to exercise dominion would get the better of him. Instead of yielding to his strength, it would stubbornly resist his efforts.

Man works and works "by the sweat of his face." But the "ground" he tries to cultivate fights back with "thorns and thistles." He feels that no matter how hard he tries, he just can't get ahead. It's never enough. His efforts are never good enough. The dust will win. It will make "dust" of him.

 Men have a natural God-given inclination to triumph and prevail (in a positive way). But because of sin, everything in life resists them and pushes back. Work pushes back. Finances push back. Even his wife and kids push back. Many men suffer with enormous feelings of failure and inadequacy. They can't possibly protect their loved ones from everything. They can't possibly provide them with enough. Sin and sickness, decay and destruction press in on every side. Though he may try his best, man just doesn't have enough fingers to plug all the holes in the dam.

Where do you see men in your sphere of relationships "battling" against the pain of manhood?

_____

_____

After two spectacularly beautiful opening chapters in Genesis about God making everything and seeing that it's good and God's amazing design and blessing on His universe, we see the horribly disfiguring consequences of sin. Sin assaults us at the very core of our beings as women and men. That which God created to display His glory and fill us with delight is now fractured, and a source of terrible pain. Only by divine intervention can what is broken be made whole. And mercifully, that's exactly what happens! We shall soon see the power of God's goodness and grace to overcome man's sinfulness and guilt.

a tragic her-story

*M*any of the emails we receive at *Revive Our Hearts* come from women who expected that saying "I do" to their Prince Charming would end in them living happily ever after. Once upon a time they had stars in their eyes. They had all kinds of dreams, hopes, and expectations.

But by the time they contact us, they are in a world of hurt, tension, and frustration. Those romantic dreams they had as younger women have turned into unfulfilled expectations, bitter disappointment, anger, and conflict. Many of these women are truly "desperate housewives," as this woman expressed:

My husband and I have been married almost thirty-five years. Last year I discovered his on-line/phone affair. We have been in counseling for a year. He keeps threatening to leave when we start getting close to talking. He believes he is entitled to private communication of any kind, at any time of day with anyone. He still considers the "friendship" with his affair partner a gift from God. He blames me for the mess his hoarding has created. He blames me for the financial problems that his spending and alcohol/drug addictions have created. He blames me for his friends not coming over. Every time I see a little progress, the verbal abuse starts again.

Another woman says:

From the very beginning of our marriage and even before it, my husband's only desire has been the fulfillment of his sexual needs. Sex was and is an idol to him. He was very demanding and would get angry when it didn't happen. . . . He was an angry, sarcastic man. His words to me were a double-edged sword, cutting to the bone and marrow. I have no memories of him building me up in Christ, only tearing me down.

Women experience heartloads of pain in marriage. And these stories are just the tip of the iceberg when it comes to how badly the male-female relationship is damaged.

You may remember hearing several years ago about the "house of horrors"—a basement dungeon where, for twenty-four years an Austrian man imprisoned his daughter, along with three of the seven children he fathered with her. He was charged with murder, slavery, rape, incest, assault, and deprivation of liberty. His battered wife had no idea he was holding their daughter captive.[2]

Men committing atrocities against women is a worldwide problem: bride burning, wife beating, widow burning, genital mutilation, infanticide, child brides, rape; mental, verbal, and physical torture; public humiliation, acid attacks, incest, pimping and prostitution, sex-slave trade, molestation, pornography, abuse, murder. The crimes are many and heinous. Instead of using their God-given strength to protect, men often use and abuse woman's vulnerabilities for their own selfish ends.

The pain of womanhood isn't trivial. It's real. It's devastating. And it cannot be ignored.

In the ministry of *Revive Our Hearts* and *Girls Gone Wise*, and at True Woman conferences, we frequently deal with women who have been hurt by men. Their stories would break your heart. And we don't just encounter these situations in our ministries; some touch us on a deeply personal level.

I (Mary) think of the friend who suspected that her husband was sexually molesting their daughter; of the friend whose pastor-husband has verbally degraded her for years; of my young friend whose boyfriend drugged and raped her; of my other friend who discovered her husband was addicted to porn and having an affair; of the friend I financed to escape her husband's blows. Even

as I type this paragraph, the tears are welling up in my eyes and my emotions are starting to churn. These are not impersonal reports and statistics. These are women I know and dearly love.

You probably have your own stories to tell—whether of your own pain, or the pain of sisters, mothers, daughters, and girlfriends. We can't shove the pain of womanhood under the carpet. It's just too real. It's just too prevalent.

How do you feel when a girlfriend confides to you about how she's been hurt by a man in her life?

I don't know about you, but when I (Mary) hear about a woman being treated poorly by a man, often my first response is anger. I get mad. I want to defend her. I want to get even. I want to strike back at the one who caused her such pain. Just last week, I held a sobbing friend and listened to how her husband (who is also a dear friend) had broken her heart. Honestly, it was all I could do not to storm over to their house, box his ears, and give him a piece of my mind. Thankfully, my husband interrupted my ranting with the gentle reminder, "Mary, he's not the real enemy here."

Women are relational beings. We relate. We empathize. So the pain of other women affects us at a deep level. We want to stand with our sisters. We want to hold them, "mother" them, kiss it all better, and fight for their happiness. We want to identify what's ailing them and help set it right.

Because God created woman "for" man; because she is the "softer," more vulnerable sex; and because of the tragic effects of the fall—many of woman's troubles throughout history stem from her relationship with man. It's tempting for us to adopt an "us-them" mentality and view men as the ultimate problem.

A few decades ago, the women behind the feminist movement did just that. They analyzed the problem of woman's pain and discontent and proposed a course of action that they thought would help.

The feminist movement analyzed the problem with male-female relation-ships. Following are some of their conclusions. Mark whether you think each statement is true (T) or false (F):

_____ Men are the problem.

_____ Patriarchy (male rule) is the problem.

_____ Woman's powerlessness is the problem.

_____ Women buckling under is the problem.

_____ Inadequate laws and penalties are the problem.

_____ Oppressive religious beliefs are the problem.

_____ Cultural conditioning is the problem.

_____ Stereotyped roles are the problem.

_____ Lack of education is the problem.

Did you find it hard to decide whether the statements analyzing the problem of the male-female relationship were true or false? Depending on how you look at it, there's a sense in which each statement is true. Certainly

these are all genuine issues and concerns. But the tough part is, there's also a sense in which each statement is false. The statements are deceptive because they mix truth and error. They aren't totally accurate, because they don't take into consideration what the root of the problem actually is.

According to Romans 3:10–18, what is the real problem behind the way men behave toward women?

Read Romans 1:29–2:1. What does this passage say to women who blame and condemn the male sex and want to lash out at men for their mistreatment of women?

The problem in the male-female relationship isn't men. It's sin. And sin is something that affects women just as much as it affects men. Men and women may sin in different ways, but the truth of the matter is that ALL have sinned and fall short of the glory of God. Women are not innocent. Women are sinners. Women can't fix sin. So we can't fix men. And we can't fix the male-female relationship. The truth is we can't even fix ourselves! (But don't despair . . . we'll soon turn our attention to Someone who can!)

The women's movement of the past century tapped into a longing to relieve the pain of womanhood and set things right. But though it identified some valid issues, it failed to address them from a biblical perspective. Instead, it encouraged women to adopt an "us-them" mentality, play the blame game, get angry, and claim the right to "do it my way!" It added fuel to the battle of the sexes by inciting women to retaliate and fight back against men.

Do women today suffer at the hands of men? For sure. But to properly address this, we need to identify the real root of the problem. As Mary's husband astutely pointed out, "Men are not the enemy here."

women's lib

> "Woe to him who says to his father, 'What have you begotten?' or to his mother, 'What have you brought to birth?' This is what the LORD says—the Holy One of Israel, and its Maker: Concerning things to come, do you question me about my children, or give me orders about the work of my hands? It is I who made the earth and created mankind upon it. My own hands stretched out the heavens; I marshaled their starry hosts."
>
> **Isaiah 45:10–12 NIV**

They called it the "Freedom Trash Can." As the random parade of women in jeans and miniskirts, braless under T-shirts, filed by, they tossed in dishcloths, oven mitts, girdles, false eyelashes, bras, copies of *Ladies Home Journal*, and various other "objects of women's oppression." Flashbulbs popped. This splashy protest of the 1968 Miss America Pageant was more newsworthy than the pageant itself.

The group of protesters auctioned off an eight-foot-eight, voluminously bosomed Miss America dummy resplendent in spangles. They trotted out a live sheep with a big bow strapped to its tail, draped it with a banner, and crowned *it* Miss America. They held up placards: "Welcome to the Miss America Cattle Auction." "I Am a Woman—Not a Toy, a Pet, or a Mascot."

Inside, television cameras zoomed in to broadcast the coronation of the pageant queen. As the pretty young woman began to speak, shouts burst out in the hall: "Down with Miss America!" "Freedom!" And then . . . a huge, white bedsheet floated slowly down from the balcony. The cameras wheeled around, and millions saw suspended on that wavy banner an unmistakable message: "WOMEN'S LIBERATION."

Thus began a feminist media extravaganza. The public watched in fascination as feminists tossed products in a toilet bowl to protest stereotyped advertising and as demonstrators staged an eleven-hour sit-in at the office of the *Ladies Home Journal*. They watched as feminists picketed the New York City Marriage License Bureau, saw the arrest of the women's libbers who broke into a pornographic publishing house, and witnessed the famous scene at New York's Plaza Hotel Oak Room where feminist leader Betty Friedan challenged the restaurant's male-only policy by taking a seat in the restaurant. (The waiter simply removed the table, rather than serve her.)

Magazines, newspapers, television, radio—every medium of public communication became engrossed with the activities and philosophy of the feminist movement. "Women's Lib" became a household term and a hot topic of conversation at nearly every gathering.[3]

the feminist solution

At the heart of the women's lib/feminist movement was the idea that to be happy, women needed to be "liberated" from age-old ideas about womanhood. They needed to "trash" the traditional view of marriage, motherhood, and morality. They needed to fight against male dominance, and seize the power and right to self-define.

Feminist activist Betty Friedan called traditional ideas about womanhood "the feminine mystique." The women's movement gained momentum when she and other women rebelled against this "mystique" and redefined womanhood based on "personal truth":

[My] words, rooted in my personal truth, led other women to their own personal truth, truth that had been hidden by the mystique. . . . [This] personal truth, led me and others to organize the women's movement. —Betty Friedan[4]

Read Isaiah 45:10–12 on the previous page. According to this passage, who has the right to decide what womanhood is about? And why?

Given what you know about the feminist movement, how was their approach flawed?

Read through the following quotes from prominent feminist thinkers:

We [women] need and can trust no other authority than our own personal truth. —Betty Friedan [5]

Women have had the power of naming stolen from us. We have not been free to use our own power to name ourselves, the world, or God . . . To exist humanly is to name the self, the world, and God . . . [Women] are now rising up to name—that is, to create—our world. —Mary Daly [6]

"Womanpower means the self-determination of women, and that means that all the baggage of paternalistic society will have to be thrown overboard." —Germaine Greer [7]

Can you identify what's wrong with these statements? Do they contain any of the same deceptive lies that Eve believed? On the list below, check off which faulty ideas they have in common:

- ☐ "I know better than God!"
- ☐ "I have the right! I have the power! I have the potential!"
- ☐ "I can decide for myself!"
- ☐ "I'll do it my way!"
- ☐ "I can solve the problem myself!"
- ☐ "It's not my fault!"
- ☐ "It's woman versus man—me against him."

Nowadays, most young women wrinkle up their noses at the word "feminism" and dismiss it as "yesterday's news"—like the go-go boots and hippy beads stashed in the back of their mother's (or grandmother's) closet. But though they reject the label, they've accepted the ideology, many of them without realizing it. Feminism has seeped into their system like an intravenous drug into the veins of an unconscious patient.

Feminism, as a cultural movement, has tapered off. This is not to say that feminism has ended. On the contrary. The only reason the feminist movement appears to have waned is that it has been so wildly successful. Feminism has transitioned from being a movement to being the prevailing mind-set of the masses. Virtually every woman is a feminist to one degree or another.

Next week, we'll talk more about the feminist movement and some of the ways in which contemporary culture's ideal for womanhood differs from God's ideal. But right now, we're going to return to Genesis one last time, to catch a glimpse of God's solution to the problem of male-female relationships.

God's solution

Read Genesis 3:20–23 on the previous page. What did Adam do after he heard God's judgment on sin? Why do you think he did this?

What signs of redemption, hope, and grace do you see in this passage?

This passage is the conclusion to a somber scene in which God has pronounced judgment and announced that the male-female relationship will be filled with pain. Man will feel the pain. Woman will feel the pain.

But the scene is not without hope. Intertwined in the curse on the Serpent, the Lord promises a Savior. Then the Lord calls the man "Adam" (3:17). It's not until after the fall that the Lord uses this proper name for him. The name is a sign that points toward Jesus Christ, the last Adam (1 Cor. 15:45)—the one who would free humanity from the ugly consequences of sin.

Adam follows the Lord's lead. He turns to his wife and names her *Eve*— "mother of all living"—a surprising choice of names, given his knowledge that "the wages of sin is death." Apparently Adam sensed the hope held out in the Lord's words. So he reached out his hand to his wife with faith that they could be redeemed and that together they could still be fruitful and life-giving.

And then, to seal the deal, the Lord did something incredible: "the Lord God made for Adam and for his wife garments of skins and clothed them" (3:21). Wow! What a powerful symbol of the grace of God! The leafy aprons the couple had stitched together were inadequate. Humanity can't cover its own sin. But God did what they were unable to do. He shed the blood of an innocent animal (a lamb?) and clothed them.[8] HE covered their sin and shame.

Do you see the symbolism here? Do you feel the rush of hope? On our own, we could never hope to fix the male-female relationship. Our "leaves" are simply inadequate. But Jesus—the Lamb of God—is willing and able to cover our sin and clothe us with His righteousness. He will help get manhood and womanhood right. Paradise *was* lost. But through Jesus Christ—and only through Him—it can be restored.

drawing it out, drawing it in...

battle of the sexes

process

The video for Week Five will help you process this week's lessons. You'll find this week's video, a downloadable outline, and many more resources at www.TrueWoman101.com/week5.

ponder

Think about the following questions. Discuss them with your friends, family, and/or small group:

1. What was amiss in Adam and Eve's behavior during Eve's interaction with the Serpent?

2. What is the sex-specific consequence of sin for women? What is the sex-specific consequence of sin for men? How did Genesis 3:16 introduce the battle of the sexes?

3. How does sin impact a woman's inclination to live according to her created design? How does it impact a man's inclination to live according to his?

4. Reread the summary of sin's judgment on women (pp. 125, 126). Describe ways in which you have personally experienced the painful reality of this judgment.

5. Are men responsible for the problem of women's pain and discontent? What is the danger in viewing men as "the enemy"?

6. Why do you think the women's movement encouraged women to do womanhood their own way? Why is the obliteration or self-definition of gender roles not the solution to the pain of womanhood?

7. Has witnessing the pain of womanhood ever incited you to blame, rail against, or devalue manhood? How can we fight against injustices toward women without demonizing men?

personalize

Use the following lined page to journal. Write down what you learned this week. Record your comments, a favorite verse, or a concept or quote that was particularly helpful or meaningful to you. Compose a prayer, letter, or poem. Jot down notes from the video or your small group session. Express your heart response to what you have studied. Personalize this week's lessons in the way that will best help you apply them to your life.

personalize it

drawing it out,
drawing it in . . .

hear me roar

L Linked arm in arm, a couple of middle-school girlfriends and I (Mary) strode down the hallway, belting out the words of Helen Reddy's 1972 chart-topping song, "I Am Woman." The words summed up our resolve. We were strong! We were invincible! We were women! We were going to roar in numbers too big to ignore! Our wisdom was born of pain! No man was ever going to keep us down again! We had paid the price! We could do anything! We were perched on the verge of womanhood. And we were confident that we would be the first generation to get the meaning of womanhood right.

As our generation got older, we pursued our rights, our careers, and a name for ourselves. We despised all relationships and responsibilities that would hold us back. We moved marriage, mothering, and homemaking from the top of our lists to the bottom —or crossed them off all together. After all, we were so much more enlightened than our fore-sisters were. The world had revolved around men, but it was our turn now. We would make it bow to our demands.

We decided that the role of wife was totally passé. Charlie's Angels seemed so much more exciting. So we redefined boundaries. We changed the rules of male-female relationships. We lashed out in self-righteous anger against male dominance. We became loud, demanding, and aggressive. We boldly pushed back against traditional definitions of gender and sexuality. We claimed our freedoms. We traded in the "Leave It to Beaver" model of womanhood for "Sex in the City." We bought into the feminist promise that woman would find happiness and fulfillment when she defined her own identity and decided for herself what life as a woman was all about.

The transformation happened so fast. In 1966, twenty-eight women gathered in Betty Friedan's hotel room to create the National Organization for Women (NOW). Roughly a hundred were involved in the 1968 Miss America protest and the demonstrations that followed. But by 1970, twenty thousand marched in solidarity at the historic New York Strike for Equality. And that's when the movement exploded.

By 1972, millions were humming the "I Am Woman" anthem. From the mid-1970s on, most students attending secular colleges were trained in feminist thought. Women's studies courses and programs mushroomed. Woman-centered analysis was integrated into virtually every discipline. Girls in grade schools were mentored in feminism with new, gender-free curriculum and textbooks. Even toddlers were inundated with kids' shows and cartoons that pushed a new, gender-neutral "Free to Be You and Me" paradigm.

"Women's Issues" became a hot topic in politics—with legislators pushing the Equal Rights Amendment, abortion rights, reproductive rights, divorce rights, affirmative action, pay equity, public day care, and other efforts to "advance" the rights of women. Billions of dollars were spent to further the feminist cause. The government established presidential commissions and state commissions and all sorts of other commissions on the status of women. Feminist research, feminist publishing, feminist groups, and feminist thought proliferated like fruit flies on a bowl of fermenting bananas.

The efforts to transform womanhood worked. Today, daughters raised in the new milieu eagerly embrace Girl Power. Girl bands like The Spice Girls and Riot Grrrls and artists like Madonna, Lady GaGa, and Katy Perry flaunt their right to self-define. They've embraced sexual power and freedom and their right to redefine gender by *kissing a girl* and liking it—gay, straight or bi, lesbian, transgendered—anything goes. Woman has the right to choose.

The feminist ideal that was once considered fringe and radical has become mainstream. It's in the air we breathe. Today's younger women can't remember a time when things were different. They assume that defining themselves—being brash, self-reliant, career-oriented, ambitious, aggressive, sexual, defiant, powerful, and fiercely individualistic—is at the core of what it means to be a woman.

Betty Friedan concluded the 1970 Strike for Equality with the blazing prediction, "After tonight, the politics of this nation will never be the same again. . . . There is no way any man, woman, or child can escape the nature of our revolution!"[1] Her words proved to be prophetic. The feminist revolution transformed our culture's view of womanhood, motherhood, marriage, and morality. No man, woman, or child in our day has been unaffected. In a single generation, everything changed. →

girls rule—boys drool

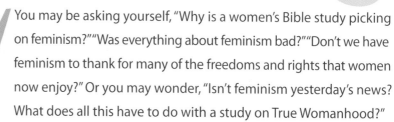

*Y*ou may be asking yourself, "Why is a women's Bible study picking on feminism?" "Was everything about feminism bad?" "Don't we have feminism to thank for many of the freedoms and rights that women now enjoy?" Or you may wonder, "Isn't feminism yesterday's news? What does all this have to do with a study on True Womanhood?"

It's important to remember that feminism is, in fact, an "-ism"—like atheism, humanism, Marxism, existentialism, or postmodernism. The "ism" indicates that we're talking about a particular philosophical theory, a doctrine, a system of principles and ideas. Feminism encompasses much more than the cultural phenomenon of the women's rights movement. It's much more than women having the right to vote, the right to pursue a career, or the right to an abortion. It's much more than the idea that women should be valued and afforded dignity and respect. It's much more than insisting on "fairness" in how the sexes are treated. Feminism is a distinct worldview with its own ideologies, values, and ways of thinking.

Did feminism identify some valid problems? Yes. Did it propose some helpful changes? It likely did. Can feminism be embraced along with our Christian faith? Absolutely not. Why not? Because it introduces a subtle (and sometimes not-so-subtle) distortion into the way we approach gender and male-female relationships. It contains truth, but it also contains some

powerful and destructive lies. And in so doing, it strikes at the very image of God and at an important earthly picture He chose to display the redemptive story. At its core, feminist philosophy is antithetical to the gospel.

Feminism is based on the wrong premise. It assumes that "patriarchy" is the ultimate cause of woman's pain. It proposes the wrong solution. It says that women have the right, the knowledge, and the power to redefine and rectify the male-female relationship. It's fueled by the wrong attitude. It encourages anger, bitterness, resentment, self-reliance, independence, arrogance, and a pitting of woman against man. It exalts the wrong

values. Power, prestige, personal attainment, and financial gain are exalted over service, sacrifice, and humility. Manhood is devalued. Morality is devalued. Marriage is devalued. Motherhood is devalued. In sum, feminism promotes ways of thinking that stand in direct opposition to the Word of God and to the beauty of His created order.

Do you agree that the philosophy of feminism is essentially incompatible with the Christian faith? Why or why not?

The reason we need to talk about feminism is that our culture upholds and promotes a feminist definition of womanhood. The word "feminist" may cause you to roll your eyeballs or stifle a yawn. You may not identify yourself as one. You may never have attended a consciousness raising group, participated in a "Take your daughter to work day," marched in a "Take back the night parade," or done anything special to acknowledge Women's History Month. You may never have listened to a feminist lecture or read a feminist book. But nonetheless, your ideas about womanhood have undoubtedly been shaped by this philosophy. And it's important for you to consider just how.

Can you identify any ways in which feminism has influenced or shaped your attitudes, values, behavior, or your thinking about womanhood?

the feminist "click"

A An article in the first issue of Gloria Steinem's feminist *MS* magazine described how a woman converts to the feminist cause when she experiences the "click" of realizing that male privilege (patriarchy) is responsible for woman's misery. The lights come on for her—her consciousness is raised—when she sees and gets angry about the fact that men are the privileged sex, and women always seem to get the short end of the stick.

"Why do I clean the toilet while you just sit around and watch football games?" CLICK! "Why do you want me to move for the sake of your career, when you're not willing to move for the sake of mine?" CLICK! "Why is it me who stays home from work when the kids are sick?" CLICK! "Why, when you do housework, do you call it 'helping' around the house?" CLICK! "Why are women expected to change their names when they get married, but men are not?" CLICK! "Why in the foreign sex trade, are men the buyers, and little girls the exploited goods?" CLICK! "Why are most CEOs male?" CLICK!

Thinking back to the consequences of the fall, explain what is legitimate about the feminist claim that "patriarchy" (the rule of men) is responsible for the unhappiness of women.

_____

_____

Now explain how putting the blame on "male-rule" subtly undermines the Bible's teaching about God's divine design for man and woman.

_____

_____

You may remember reading about "Nicole" back in Week One. Nicole said she had experienced the feminist *click* and had, for many years, been angry at men. But as she listened to the speakers at True Woman, she experienced another, more powerful *click*. Her new "aha" was the realization that the ultimate purpose of manhood and womanhood was to display the story of the gospel; and that sin is responsible for pitting man against woman and marring the beauty of God's divine design.

"Be angry and do not sin; do not let the sun go down on your anger, and give no opportunity to the devil. . . . Let all bitterness and wrath and anger and clamor and slander be put away from you, along with all malice. Be kind to one another, tenderhearted, forgiving one another, as God in Christ forgave you."

Ephesians 4:26–27, 31–32

"See to it that no one fails to obtain the grace of God; that no 'root of bitterness' springs up and causes trouble, and by it many become defiled."

Hebrews 12:15

Instead of anger, this *click* led to repentance. Nicole repented of her hard-heartedness, her bitterness, her spirit of rebellion, her attempts to manipulate and control, and all the other ways in which she had bought into the feminist lie and contributed to the problem.

The feminist *click* points the finger of blame at "patriarchal" role differences, and incites anger against men. In fact, one of the basic tools of the early feminist movement was the technique of "Consciousness Raising" (CR). The slogan behind CR is: "Speak bitterness to recall bitterness; speak pain to recall pain." In other words, if you can get a woman to talk about her hurt, the women who listen will empathize, and will in turn recall and share their own hurt. When anger and bitterness is shared back and forth like this, it escalates and becomes a powerful tool to get women involved in the feminist cause.

The early feminist movement stirred up bitterness and discontent among a whole generation of women, most of whom had never before seen themselves as oppressed victims. Those seeds took root and produced a bumper crop of angry women intent on redressing all the ill treatment they had received at the hands of men and a male-dominated culture.

What's the problem with anger? Read the verse in the margin of the previous page. In the space below, make a list of reasons why anger can be counterproductive.

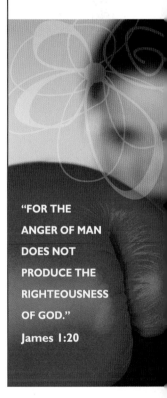

"FOR THE ANGER OF MAN DOES NOT PRODUCE THE RIGHTEOUSNESS OF GOD."
James 1:20

Do you remember how I (Mary) reacted when I found out that a married male friend had betrayed his wife? I got angry and wanted to lash out at him. Anger is a natural but dangerous emotional response. There is such a thing as righteous anger. Anger is not sin, but if it's misdirected or prolonged, it can quickly lead to sin.

For Nicole, which response was more likely to result in improved relationships? Her anger at men for the way in which they had failed? Or her repentance for the way in which she had failed? Why?

Are you angry at some man for the way he has treated you? Based on the verses in the margin of the previous page, how does God want you to respond? How does the gospel of Christ motivate and enable that kind of response?

girls gone wild effect

*W*hen Miss America 1968 appeared in an evening gown and swimwear at the bequest of *men*, feminism identified her as "exploited." But when Miss USA 2010 posed for some sexy pornlike bedroom photos, and boldly rejected social convention by entering and winning top honors in a pole dancing competition—and did so under the guise of *woman's* freedom, power, and right to self-define—not one feminist organization protested, paraded livestock, set up a trash can, or even uttered a peep.

What could they say? This young woman was embracing and living out feminism's core values. Given a feminist belief system, they had no choice but to concede that her brash, immoral behavior was "empowered."

These days, young women have the mind-set that sexual lewdness equals female empowerment. Newsweek dubbed this "The Girls Gone Wild Effect."[2] The label was derived from Joe Francis's Girls Gone Wild

video empire, which he built by visiting beaches, nightclubs, and parties across America and getting "everyday" college-age women to expose themselves for the sake of a dare and a T-shirt. When asked why he thought thousands of young women were so eager to exhibit themselves for his cameras, so willing to objectify themselves in exchange for trucker hats and tank tops, Francis simply said "It's empowering. It's freedom."[3]

Joe Francis sees the Girl Gone Wild phenomenon as the ultimate expression of feminism. Muzi Mei, the Carrie Bradshaw of Beijing who became a superstar by blogging about her sexual conquests, agrees. She told a reporter, "I express my freedom through sex. It's my life, and I can do what I want."[4] Young, third wave feminists revel in the fact that "showing herself in sexual ways makes a woman feel powerful and men powerless."[5]

Due to the feminist call for women to throw off traditional, Judeo-Christian restrictions and define themselves however they wish, culture now deems it acceptable and even *good* for women to be "bad." Today, a girl is inundated with the idea that it's nice to be naughty—to be a good woman, she needs to embrace a bit of badness. The boundary between right and wrong has become virtually indistinct.

Although our culture encourages women to blur the distinction, the Bible is clear about what type of behavior is right and what type is wrong. It doesn't support the idea that being bad is a good thing.

In Proverbs 7, a father gives his young son instructions on how to spot a "bad girl." His cautionary tale paints a picture of a typical Girl Gone Wild. In this particular narrative, she is depicted as a young, married, religious woman—an ordinary, average, "typical" Jane Doe you could meet at the church down the street. But she could be any woman: young, old, single, married, divorced, widowed, childless; a mother, a teenager, a grandma . . . whatever.

The point of the story isn't her age or marital status. It's about the foolish ("wild") characteristics she displays. As you'll soon see, these characteristics could show up in a woman of any age, of any marital status, at any stage of life.

Read Proverbs 7:6–27 in your Bible. In the space below, jot down several behaviors and characteristics of the Wild Thing that stand out to you in this story.

_____

_____

_____

What do these qualities reveal about the Wild Thing's heart and her relationship with the Lord?

_____

_____

The Wild Thing of Proverbs 7 obviously tried to keep her rendezvous under wraps. She would have been embarrassed if people found out about her conduct. In our culture, things are quite different. In times past, people frowned at the idea of a girl going wild, but now, they support woman's choice to do so—in fact, they encourage her to proudly flaunt her naughty side.

How does the description of the "bad girl" in Proverbs 7 compare to the ideal for womanhood upheld today? Mark whether *our culture* considers each descriptor to be a **D**esirable, **A**cceptable, or **U**nacceptable trait for women:

	D	A	U
She thumbs her nose at what's considered "proper".			
She dresses provocatively.			
She's crafty and manipulative.			
She insists on getting her own way.			
She's defiant and rebellious.			
She disdains/devalues homemaking.			
She wants to be out where the action is.			
She's the initiator in male-female relationships.			
She's flirtatious.			
She's sexually aggressive.			
She's sassy and brash.			
She is spiritual, but sets her own standards.			
She goes after what she wants, even if it's off bounds.			
She's a shopaholic with designer-label desire.			
She is sensual and breaks sexual taboos.			
She feels entitled to delight herself as she sees fit.			
She blames her man for the ways in which he fails.			
She gets back at him for hurting her.			
She doesn't have a high regard for marriage.			
She's a smooth-talker who can easily control a guy.			
She has had several sexual partners.			
She lays men low.			

What can you conclude about how the Bible's ideal for womanhood compares to today's ideal?

_____

_____

   When I (Nancy) read Proverbs 7, in my mind's eye I see women I know who, though they are "churched" and consider themselves to be believers, have made choices that are more consistent with the world's way of thinking than with the Word of God.

   I think of a married woman I spoke with who was in an adulterous relationship with a colleague at the Christian ministry where she worked. Or the mother of six children who wrote me a note at a conference where I spoke, sharing that she was spending twelve to eighteen hours a day online, and was considering leaving her family for a man she had met on the Internet.

   I think of women who have been influenced by the world's model of womanhood. They lack discernment and discretion; they see nothing wrong with being flirtatious, using suggestive or coarse language, carrying on covert Facebook exchanges with old boyfriends, wearing clothing that exposes or emphasizes private parts of the body, or numerous other "wild" patterns. In some cases, they are ignorant or naïve of what the Bible teaches. In other cases, they are more interested in fitting into the world than in honoring and reflecting the Lord.

   Some of them have already shipwrecked their lives and the lives of others; others may be well on the path to doing so.

According to Proverbs 5:5–6, why did this Wild Thing go astray?

_____

_____

What kind of influence/impact does the Wild Thing's life have on others (her husband, other men, other women, her children)?

_____

_____

Review the descriptors of wildness on the previous page. Put a check mark beside any that are characteristic of you.

→ **If it expresses the desire of your heart**, ask the Lord to change you into a wise woman in every area of your life.

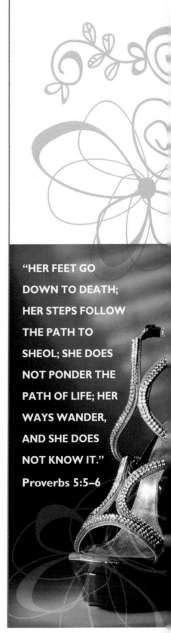

"HER FEET GO DOWN TO DEATH; HER STEPS FOLLOW THE PATH TO SHEOL; SHE DOES NOT PONDER THE PATH OF LIFE; HER WAYS WANDER, AND SHE DOES NOT KNOW IT."
Proverbs 5:5–6

the dinner party

*J*udy Chicago's *The Dinner Party* is the most famous icon of feminist art. It premiered in San Francisco in 1979 and toured sixteen venues in six countries on three continents, to a viewing audience of over a million. Since 2007 it's been on permanent exhibition in the Elizabeth A. Sackler Center for Feminist Art at the Brooklyn Museum in New York City.

Chicago's display consists of a massive banquet table in the shape of an equilateral triangle. The triangular shape symbolizes the female. The equilateral sides represent equality. Along each side are thirteen place settings. The number mockingly emulates the most lauded dinner party ever—that of Christ and His twelve disciples at the Last Supper. Chicago said she wanted to reinterpret that all-male event so that women, and not men, were the honored guests.

Each of the thirty-nine table settings graphically, perversely depicts private body parts of a notable woman from history or mythology, ranging from a primordial goddess to the American painter Georgia O'Keefe. The table stands on a floor of white ceramic tiles, on which a further 999 names of women are written in gold. According to its designer, *"The Dinner Party* expresses the belief and hope that once reverence for the feminine is re-established on Earth, a balance will be restored to human existence and everywhere will be Eden once again."[6]

Chicago's choice to position women around a table acknowledges what happens when feminists get together with girlfriends to vent, fuel bitterness, and organize for political change. Women's dinner parties were a powerful tool to raise consciousness and advance the feminist cause. Chicago hoped *The Dinner Party* would compel people to accept the real-life feminist invitation. She hoped they'd accept a chair at the table of feminism, work to rid the world of patriarchy, and put power securely in the hands of women. She promised if they did, they'd be sure to help create paradise!

The dinner party theme brings to mind two women in the Bible who were also extremely eager to get people to attend their parties. Two chapters after the story of the Wild Thing of Proverbs 7, a personification of wisdom, Lady Wise, extends an invitation for women to attend her feast. But hers is not

the only, nor the loudest, party in town. Lady Wild is also throwing a big bash. She wants women to accept *her* invitation. Lady Wild promises that at her table, they'll have an absolutely great time!

Read Proverbs 9:1–6, 10, 13–18 in your Bible. At the bottom of each invitation, fill in the blank to indicate whether the invitation was extended by Lady Wild or Wise.

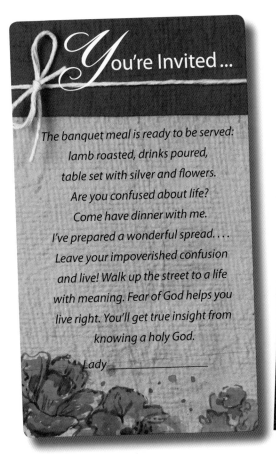

You're Invited...

The banquet meal is ready to be served:
lamb roasted, drinks poured,
table set with silver and flowers.
Are you confused about life?
Come have dinner with me.
I've prepared a wonderful spread. . . .
Leave your impoverished confusion
and live! Walk up the street to a life
with meaning. Fear of God helps you
live right. You'll get true insight from
knowing a holy God.

Lady_____

You're Invited . . .

Are you confused about life, don't know what's going on? Steal off with me; I'll show you a good time! Don't worry about all those silly "don't eat" rules. Just indulge! You deserve to have fun, don't you? Remember "What happens at the party stays at the party." No one will ever know. I guarantee you'll have the time of your life!

Lady_____

Which party sounds like more fun? Why?

_____

_____

Judy Chicago crossed Jesus off her guest list. She didn't want Him sitting at her table. Lady Wild does the same thing. The first thing we can observe about Lady Wild's invitation in Proverbs 9:13–17 is that it doesn't mention the Lord; she leaves Him totally out of the picture. She wants her guests to indulge without His interference.

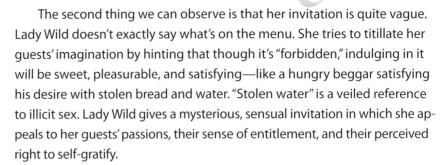

The second thing we can observe is that her invitation is quite vague. Lady Wild doesn't exactly say what's on the menu. She tries to titillate her guests' imagination by hinting that though it's "forbidden," indulging in it will be sweet, pleasurable, and satisfying—like a hungry beggar satisfying his desire with stolen bread and water. "Stolen water" is a veiled reference to illicit sex. Lady Wild gives a mysterious, sensual invitation in which she appeals to her guests' passions, their sense of entitlement, and their perceived right to self-gratify.

Verse 13 mentions three of Lady Wild's characteristics:

- She's loud.
- She's seductive.
- She knows nothing.

"Loud" means she's riotous. She makes a lot of noise and clamors for attention; she's turbulent, subject to passionate and extreme mood swings. "Seductive" means she is without safeguard or restraint; she has no moral fiber to resist temptation; she is sensual and she is persuasive. "Knows nothing" literally means "does not know what" (is right and proper); she is willfully and persistently ignorant; she recklessly ignores the consequences of her conduct.

Based on these characteristics, how do you think Lady Wild might try to get you to attend her dinner party? Check all the statements that are true.

- ☐ She'll clamor to get my attention.
- ☐ She'll incessantly badger and nag.
- ☐ She'll play on my emotions.
- ☐ She'll manipulate and sweet-talk.
- ☐ She'll be extremely persuasive and enticing.
- ☐ She'll make sin sound fascinating and enjoyable.
- ☐ She'll be honest and up-front.
- ☐ She'll intentionally conceal and mislead.

Lady Wild entices guests to come to her party in the same way that the Serpent enticed Eve to his. Satan convinced Eve that wildness was attractive, harmless, and extremely promising. "Nothing bad will happen!"

This may be the most fundamental lie Satan tells us about sin. God had said to Adam, "If you eat the fruit of this tree, you will die" (see Gen. 2:17). The command was clear: "Don't eat." The consequence for disobedience was equally clear: "You will die."

After Satan raised a question about the goodness of God in giving such a mandate and whether God in fact had the right to control Eve's life, he proceeded to challenge the consequence. He did so with a direct, frontal attack on the Word of God: "You will not surely die!" (Gen. 3:4).

The reason women disobey God and party with Lady Wild is that they believe they can get away with it. The Enemy causes us to believe that:

- "This won't result in any trouble."
- "I can manage it."
- "No one will ever know."
- "I won't reap what I sow."
- "The choices I make won't have any bad consequences."
- "I can play with fire and not get burned."

We must keep reminding ourselves that Satan is a liar. He tells us that wildness is fun, natural, desirable, pleasurable, gratifying, fascinating, and exhilarating—and above all, that it won't do us any harm. But it's a lie.

According to Proverbs 9:18, what actually happens to those who accept the invitation to dine at Lady Wild's table?

Lady Wild's invitation is compelling and alluring. Wildness seems like it will be harmless and so much fun. But the truth is, saying yes will slowly kill you on the inside. It will lead to spiritual death.

→ **Close today's lesson in prayer**. Ask the Lord to forgive you for the times you've indulged at Lady Wild's table. Ask Him to give you the discernment and strength to say no to future invitations, and to respond to the invitation of Lady Wise instead.

smart girls get more

S "Smart Girls Get More" is a wildly successful ad campaign that promotes the United Kingdom's bestselling women's magazine, *More*. The message shouts from billboards, buses, TV commercials, radio spots, sponsorships, and competitions. It inundates British women with the idea that if they are smart, they will get *more*—more men, more sex, more celebrity gossip, more beauty, more fashion, more products, more delicacies, and, of course, more of the magazine that gives them all the latest and greatest information on these pleasures. "Cuz Smart Girls Get More!"

Yesterday, we compared two dinner party invitations—one issued by Lady Wise and the other by Lady Wild. Lady Wild drops all sorts of seductive hints about how great her wild party will be. But though she's persuasive, her words are empty. And ultimately, so is her table. Truth is, she has no food. She's done nothing to prepare. Her guests will have to steal water and bread in an attempt to alleviate their hunger and thirst. Lady Wild won't spend a penny to feed them. She won't lift a finger to serve them.

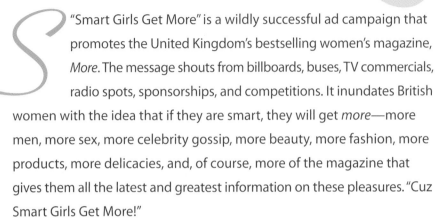

Not only that, she conveniently neglects to tell invitees about all the previous guests who have wasted away at her table, and that she's in the habit of hoarding their old skeletons. Lady Wild has no substance to back up her style. Her party is a dud. It stinks! Reeks of death.

The Bible says that girls who respond to Lady Wise get so much more than the women who respond to Lady Wild's invitation. The fact is, "*wise* girls get more" of what really matters for this life and the next! Proverbs 9 describes the lengths to which Lady Wise goes to prepare a banquet for her guests. Wisdom builds a spacious, seven-columned house and carves the intricate pillars by hand. She provides meat from her field, choice wine from her cellar, fresh-baked bread from her ovens. She fusses over the table setting and décor. She spends days in the kitchen, mixing up her favorite recipes. She works hard. She attends to every detail. She spares no expense. She wants her guests to enjoy the best and most satisfying dinner party of their lives.

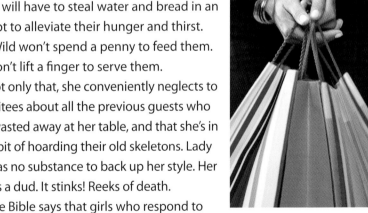

Today we are going to look at another passage that gives us more insight into the ways of Lady Wise. Read Proverbs 8:1–21 and answer the following questions:

Why should you trust/choose Lady Wise over Lady Wild (vv. 6–11)?

_____

_____

What four things will you get when you hang out with Lady Wise (v. 14)?

_____

_____

Verses 18–21 speak of "riches" and "fruit" received by those who say yes to wisdom. Put a check next to the kind of riches you think you can count on if you choose the pathway of wisdom:

- ☐ a good-paying job doing something you love to do
- ☐ freedom from physical pain/life-threatening diseases
- ☐ integrity of heart
- ☐ a right relationship with God
- ☐ provision of all your wants
- ☐ provision of all your needs
- ☐ a lovely house in a decent neighborhood
- ☐ God's guidance for your life
- ☐ social popularity
- ☐ meaningful fellowship with others who are wise
- ☐ a godly husband and children
- ☐ discernment
- ☐ discretion

- ☐ great health insurance and retirement benefits
- ☐ fruitful ministry in others' lives
- ☐ the fruit of the Spirit
- ☐ friendship/intimacy with God
- ☐ grace to respond to difficult people
- ☐ freedom from problems or pain
- ☐ grace to persevere through difficult circumstances
- ☐ hope for the future
- ☐ the peace of God
- ☐ a figure like a model
- ☐ freedom from guilt
- ☐ freedom from fear
- ☐ a clear conscience

smarten up!

You need to be smart when it comes to the messages you listen to. Culture promotes a way of thinking about womanhood that is decidedly feminist. Its solution to the battle of the sexes is to dismantle patriarchy, and in the process, undermine and dismantle God's divine design. How does it do this? By convincing women that they have the right to self-define. We hope you've seen that this strategy of Satan is as old as time.

Eve fell for it. She was deceived by the idea that God didn't have her best interests at heart, that she could come up with a better way, and that there was no harm in trying. It didn't work for Eve. It didn't work for the Wild Thing of Proverbs 7. And it won't work for you.

The Bible boils it down for us. It says that if we listen to God, we will go wise. But if we don't listen to Him, we will go wild. And the consequence of increased wildness is increased pain and dysfunction. You only have to look at the history of feminism to see that this is the case. Many feminists had the best of intentions. At the core, they desired to find a solution to the age-old problem of sin and the pain of womanhood. But when they moved away from God's design instead of moving toward it, they exacerbated the very problem they were trying to solve.

In October 2009, *Time* magazine devoted an entire issue to "The State of the American Woman." One writer pointed out that, ironically, as women have gained more education, more economic independence, more power, and more freedom, they have become less and less happy. According to evidence gathered by numerous surveys, they are unhappier now than when the feminist movement set about to solve the problem of women's unhappiness.[7] Clearly, the new model of womanhood is even less fulfilling than the old one was.

"Listen to me: blessed are those who keep my ways. Hear instruction and be wise, and do not neglect it. Blessed is the one who listens to me, watching daily at my gates, waiting beside my doors. For whoever finds me finds life and obtains favor from the LORD...."

Proverbs 8:32–35

"But he who fails to find me injures himself; all who hate me love death."

Proverbs 8:36

"Wisdom is better than jewels, and all that you may desire cannot compare with her."

Proverbs 8:11

The solution isn't to try to rewind the clock to the 1950s, and squeeze women back into that culture's "Leave It to Beaver" stereotype. No. The solution —the biblical solution—is to embrace the Word of God, and ask Him to help us figure out how to live out His divine design in *this* culture. Truly "smart girls" know that the place to get more know-how, freedom, and joy is in a relationship with Christ—the One "in whom are hidden all the treasures of wisdom and knowledge" (Col. 2:3).

Refer to Proverbs 8:32–35 to complete the following chart:

If you do this ...	This will be the result ...

According to Proverbs 8:36, what will be the outcome if you fail to pursue the wisdom found in Christ?

_____

_____

In response to Proverbs 8:11, write a brief prayer in the space below, agreeing with God about the value of wisdom and expressing your desire to be filled with His wisdom.

_____

_____

_____

a taste for it

*T*he outdoor markets in Thailand offer a fascinating shopping experience. They're colorful, busy, and chaotic, with narrow mazes of alleyways crammed with side-to-side and back-to-back stalls, selling everything from vegetables, spices, and fruits, to ornate teak curiosities, handicrafts, textiles, and silks, to cheap shoes and designer rip-offs.

I (Mary) will never forget visiting the Night Bazaar, or Kad Luang (Royal Market), in Chiang Mai. It was there that I first encountered the Thai affinity for creepy crawlies. Deep-fried, giant water bugs are one of the most popular snacks sold in Thailand. Street vendors also offer an assortment of other munchies: locusts, beetles, bamboo worms, larvae-on-a-stick, and scorpion-on-a-stick. Most are served crispy, with a light coating of Thai pepper powder or fish paste.

At one such stall, an old, wrinkled woman, with a massive smile beaming out from under her bamboo hat, beckoned me to indulge. I could see a Thai man walking away from the stall, biting the head and pincers off a palm-sized arthropod. Another laughed and chatted with a friend as he counted out twenty *baht* for a bag of grasshoppers, and immediately started popping them into his mouth. Both men were obviously enjoying the crunchy delicacies. But for me, it felt like "Fear Factor." The thought of eating insects made me gag. I just couldn't bring myself to do it.

I've decided that my aversion to eating bugs has little to do with how good they actually taste or how nutritious they may be. It has much more to do with my background and nationality. The maggots that Thai people love are a Canadian's nightmare. And this is the case for many national culinary treats: Chinese eat bird's nest soup, Koreans eat squirming live octopus, Indonesians drink coffee made from the excrement of the catlike luwak, Icelanders eat raw puffin heart, Japanese eat tuna eyeballs, ranchers in Colorado eat prairie oysters (deep-fried bull testicles), Cambodians eat balut (eggs containing fully developed chicken embryos), and Texans eat chicken-fried steak. (Really?!)

> "...just as Sarah obeyed Abraham, calling him lord. You have become her children when you do good and are not frightened by anything alarming."
>
> **1 Peter 3:6** HCSB

Each of these foods, while considered weird, bizarre, and disgusting to me, is considered tasty and delectable in certain countries and cultures. My lack of affinity has to do with my foreign nationality. It has to do with how my heritage and upbringing have affected my tastes. I think eating cockroaches is repulsive because most people in Canada think that eating cockroaches is repulsive. It's a scary thought because the idea is so foreign and unfamiliar to me.

For many women, Scripture's instruction on gender is like that. In fact, one passage specifically addresses the need for women to openly face their fears about biblical womanhood.

Read 1 Peter 3:1–7 in your Bible. What positive or negative thoughts or emotions does this passage prompt in you?

Why do you think the concept of "biblical womanhood" triggers a "Fear Factor" for some women?

At times, both of us have struggled with this passage in our journey to grasp and embrace our true womanhood. As a younger woman, this passage conjured up in my (Nancy's) mind an image of a mousy woman with a perpetually demure disposition—a woman who just nodded her head and rarely expressed her thoughts or perspective. In fact, I knew a few women I thought of as godly, who were extremely reserved; they seemed to me to exemplify what it meant to have a "meek and quiet" spirit. But as much as I respected them, I felt frustrated, because I knew I just was not wired that way. If that is what it looked like to be a godly woman, it seemed like an impossible ideal, one I would never be able to attain, apart from a "personality transplant"!

And I (Mary) really used to dislike this passage—when I was in my twenties, it made the hair on the back of my neck stand on end. Back then, reading it felt like sticking my face in a plate of creepy crawlies.

But now, thirty years later, we both feel quite differently. We have grown to love and appreciate this passage. And—to use the analogy of Mary's (and Nancy's!) aversion to scorpion-on-a-stick—we think the change of perspective is due to the fact that another (heavenly) country has claimed our allegiance. As a result, our tastes have changed. What once seemed bizarre and distasteful is now delectable to us and highly cherished.

All this week, we've been considering how our ideas about womanhood have been shaped by Western culture. Feminism has been the featured item on our culture's menu for the past several decades. It's been the staple of our diets. It's become familiar to us. We're used to it. We're used to seeing it cooked up. We're used to watching it be set on our tables. We're used to having it dished out. We're used to seeing it on our plates. We're used to the way it smells. We're used to its consistency and color. We're used to biting into it. We're used to feeling its texture in our mouths. We're used to the way it tastes. We're used to chewing it. We're used to swallowing it. Its flavor doesn't seem odd or distasteful. Feminist ideas about womanhood seem absolutely normal because they are common to this country.

You may not be as familiar with the Bible's food. Its teaching on gender serves up the delicacy of a different kingdom. The textures, smells, colors, and flavors are different, and may be something you've not experienced before. Biblical womanhood is foreign to modern culture (and to fallen human nature). So don't be surprised if it presents you with a bit of a fear factor, as it once did for us.

What does the world say will likely happen to you if you embrace the Bible's teachings about womanhood?

_____

_____

How do you feel about these prospects?

_____

_____

"But let your adorning be the hidden person of the heart with the imperishable beauty of a gentle and quiet spirit, which in God's sight is very precious."

I Peter 3:4

We've heard all sorts of dismal prognoses about what will happen to women who decide to push back from the table of wildness and embrace God's vision for womanhood instead. You've probably heard (or thought) them too:

You'll become a doormat. You'll be a ditz. You'll lose brain cells. You'll encourage abuse. You'll become passive. You'll lose your opinion. You'll lose your voice. You'll lose your personality. You'll end up with twenty kids and counting. You'll turn into a frump. You'll turn into a girlie girl. You'll turn into a Stepford wife. You'll waste your potential. You'll be taken advantage of. You'll lose out. You'll become a slave. You'll be boring. You'll always get the short end of the stick. You'll be unfulfilled. You'll be sorry! (Strike up the scary organ music . . . !)

Sorry, but those dire threats are just plain silly. The truth is, as anxious as we might be about what could happen if we fully follow the Lord, we should be far more concerned about what will happen if we don't! Trusting the wisdom of our good, loving heavenly Father is safer and far more attractive than trusting Satan's deceptive sales pitch and stepping out on our own.

According to 1 Peter 3:4, how does the Lord feel about true womanhood?

_____

_____

How do you need to adjust your attitude toward womanhood so that it matches His?

_____

_____

→ **Are you ready for a True Woman total makeover?** We hope this week's lessons have helped you see how culture has influenced your thoughts about womanhood. We hope you've decided to respond positively to the invitation of Lady Wise, face your fears, and develop a greater taste for godliness. Next week, we'll take a look at several New Testament passages about God's divine design. We think you'll see that womanhood is indeed a precious and beautiful thing.

drawing it out,
drawing it in...

hear me roar

process

The video for Week Six will help you process this week's lessons. You'll find this week's video, a downloadable outline, and many more resources at www.TrueWoman101.com/week6.

ponder

Think about the following questions. Discuss them with your friends, family, and/or small group:

1. Can you think of some examples of friends, teachers, curriculum, TV programs, books, or other things that have specifically pushed feminist ideas at you? What part of the message was good? What part of the message was counter to God's Word and ways? In what ways has feminism shaped your thinking?

2. What subtle distortions does feminism introduce into the way we approach gender and male-female relationships?

3. Review the description of the Wild Thing of Proverbs 7 listed on page 146. How does the ideal for womanhood in Scripture compare to today's ideal? Which ideal do you find more desirable? Why?

4. Which of the techniques listed on page 150 has Lady Wild used to get you to attend her party? Why should you trust and choose the invitation of Lady Wise over Lady Wild?

5. Why do you think that as women have gained more education, more economic independence, more power, and more freedom, they have become less and less happy?

6. Why do you think the concept of true womanhood presents a "Fear Factor" for some women? How do you need to adjust your attitude toward womanhood so that it's more in line with how the Lord views it?

personalize

Use the following lined page to journal. Write down what you learned this week. Record your thoughts, comments, favorite verse, or an impactful idea or quote. Compose a prayer, letter, or poem. Jot down notes from the video or your small group session. We've provided this space so that you can personalize this week's lessons in the way that will best help you apply them to your life.

personalize it

drawing it out,
drawing it in . . .

total makeover

Don't you love those "before" and "after" pictures of someone or something that's received a total makeover? The idea of getting a makeover is so compelling that dozens of TV reality shows are based on the concept.

In one of the most popular shows, TLC's "What Not to Wear," friends, family, or coworkers nominate a candidate whom they consider poorly dressed and in need of a fashion makeover. Cameras secretly follow her, videotaping her fashion faux pas.

Fashion Police Stacy London and Clinton Kelly review the footage and provide sarcastic commentary as to why the nominee's wardrobe is unflattering ("mom-jeans"), unsightly (mismatched patterns), or out-of-date (purchased in the 1980s). Nominators knowingly giggle, groan, and roll their eyeballs. Then, the entire group sets out to ambush the unsuspecting "fashion victim."

Stacey and Clinton offer the surprised candidate $5000 for a new wardrobe—on the condition that she allows them to critique (and in most cases throw out) her existing wardrobe, and that she shops by their "rules." If she agrees, she's brought to New York City for an entire week of evaluation, shopping, and hair and makeup styling.

The show climaxes in the big "reveal." Back in her hometown, supporters eagerly wait. They break out in oohs and ahhs and thunderous applause as the made-over woman makes her entrance. Beaming from ear-to-ear, she twirls around to show off the beauty of her new-

and-improved style. She's a "new woman." As the show ends, she gives testimony as to how the makeover has transformed not only her appearance but also her self-image and her life.

Other types of makeovers follow the same basic script. Houses are made over. Rooms are made over. Yards are made over. Restaurants are made over. Cars are made over. Bodies are made over. Bad habits are made over. Relationships are made over. In each case, experts intervene to remake something plain, unattractive, or dysfunctional into something beautiful and beneficial. They take something that's "yuck" or "ho-hum" and transform it into a "Wow!" Their skillful intervention reveals and optimizes its true potential.

One of the interesting things about TV makeovers is watching the participants' reaction to the process. Some are eager and cooperative. Others are skeptical and resistant. The occasional one is downright combative and hostile. Once, when Stacy and Clinton encountered a woman who was particularly unyielding and antagonistic, Stacy threw up her hands in exasperation and countered, "Who are the fashion experts here? Do you really think you know more than we do? Why don't you trust us? We know what we're doing!"

The woman badly needed a makeover. That was clear. But she was blind to her own shortcomings, so Stacey and Clinton faced resistance when they pointed them out. She finally, begrudgingly, admitted that they knew more about fashion than she did, and acquiesced to their opinion. In the end, she was glad she did. The transformation was amazing! When an expert directs the makeover, it usually is.

For the past two weeks, we've been considering how sin damaged and marred the beauty of true womanhood. Womanhood needs a total makeover. Culture tried to give it one. But it failed miserably. That's because it didn't consult the right expert. It didn't enlist the help of the only One who has the knowledge and power to set things right.

God's Son, Jesus Christ, died in order to break the power of sin's grip on us. He's the ultimate makeover artist. He enables us to reclaim the beauty of who God created us to be. He's the expert on manhood and womanhood. In this week's lessons, we'll be looking at how the gospel of Christ redeems (rescues, saves, and makes over) true womanhood from the ugliness of sin.

Jesus Christ wants to restyle your womanhood and teach you how to "dress" according to God's divine design. Whether you're eager, skeptical, or even antagonistic, you're undeniably a candidate for a total makeover. The Lord wants you to trust Him, shop by His "rules," let Him cut, snip, and redirect your "look." If you do, He'll give you a dramatic makeover and transform your womanhood into a thing of beauty. The "before" and "after" pictures will be amazing, because Jesus Christ will turn your "ho-hum" into a "Wow!"—and the "new woman" will bear a striking resemblance to Him! $\rightarrow$

beautiful design

Every year, hundreds of leading corporations vie for the GOOD DESIGN Award, which is conferred annually by the Chicago Athenaeum Museum of Architecture and Design. As implied by its name, the award recognizes commercial products that excel by having a good design. The international recognition was founded in 1950 by three architects. But did you know that at the dawn of creation, God handed out His own "Good Design" awards?

God created light, and then acknowledged that the light was "good" (Gen. 1:4). "Good" was also the award He gave to the newly created land and sea, vegetation, sun, moon and stars, sea creatures and birds, beasts of the earth, livestock, and things that creep on the ground. All of these things merited His "Good Design" award.

Only once did God determine that the design of something was *not* good. It happened before He created woman. God said it was *"not good"* that man should be alone (Gen. 2:18). Something was missing. The design was incomplete. Without woman, the story just didn't make sense.

How could a man express the story of Christ and the church without a bride? How could he showcase the relationship? How could he depict the union? How could he be fruitful without her? He couldn't.

And how could the man portray the love Christ would have for His bride, and how could that bride's respectful and adoring submission to Christ be pictured, unless the woman was brought to the man?

Woman was vital to the story line. Without her, there would be no story, and no one to hear it either. The creation of the woman provided a vital picture of Christ's bride.

After God created woman, things were good again. In fact, they were even better than good. In God's own assessment, things were *VERY good* (Gen. 1:31)! His creation of manhood, womanhood, and marriage—and that to which it pointed—merited the highest possible GOOD DESIGN award.

Read the verses from Psalms found in the margin on page 164. What can you conclude about God's design for womanhood? Check all that apply:

- ☐ Womanhood is the work of God's hand.
- ☐ God's design for womanhood is great.
- ☐ God's design for womanhood is splendid and majestic.
- ☐ God's design for womanhood is faithful and just.
- ☐ God's design for womanhood is remarkable.
- ☐ God's design for womanhood is wonderful.
- ☐ God's design for womanhood is wise.
- ☐ God's design for womanhood is delightful.
- ☐ God's design for womanhood is magnificent.
- ☐ God's design for womanhood is profound.

Did you check all the boxes? Do you believe, deep in your heart of hearts, that God's design for womanhood is all these things? Do you believe it's delightful? Do you believe it's remarkable? Do you believe it's truly wonderful?

While we have both always believed that womanhood was the work of God's hand, and therefore inherently right, we didn't always feel that it was "great" or "splendid." There was a time when the thought of living by His design felt about as appealing as getting our teeth drilled—perhaps the right or necessary thing to do, but certainly not something to get excited about. We are so grateful that God has gently corrected our faulty thinking.

Summarize why God's design for womanhood is beautiful and good:

_____

_____

poetic masterpiece

Man and woman are the work of God's hands (Isa. 64:8). They are His "workmanship." The Greek word used here is *poiema*; it's the word from which we get our English word "poem." It means "work" or "creation" and is associated specifically with God's activity. *Poiema* is only used twice in the New Testament—in Romans 1:20 and in Ephesians 2:10. The first use of this term points to God's handiwork in His creation of the universe, including man and woman, while the second refers to His marvelous work in redeeming humanity from sin.

In the verses in the margin, circle the word "poiema."

All of creation (including male and female) was designed to showcase God's eternal power and divine nature (Rom. 1:19–20). Sadly, His beautiful design for male and female (along with everything else in this world) was damaged by sin. But it became God's masterpiece when He re-created it through Jesus Christ (Eph. 2:10). Through the cross, Christ defeated the power of Satan and sin, so manhood and womanhood can once again display the magnificent beauty of His created design.

Paul says, *"Thanks be to God, that you who were once slaves of sin have become obedient from the heart to the standard of teaching to which you were committed"* (Rom. 6:17).

Which "standard of teaching" about gender do you think God wants you to obey?

- ☐ The standard established in God's created design and revealed in His Word
- ☐ The standard displayed in sin's twisted design
- ☐ The standard upheld in culture's gender-neutral design

New Testament teaching on gender reinforces the roles that were established at creation. New life in Jesus gives us the freedom and power to live according to this divine design. Through the power of the Holy Spirit, we can delight in the differences between man and woman, live in accordance with Scripture's standards, and allow our manhood and womanhood to recite God's magnificent poem.

restoring the masterpiece

One of the greatest masterpieces of the Italian Renaissance, the *Madonna del Cardellino,* was painted by Raphael in 1505 for the wedding of his friend, a wealthy Florentine merchant. Unfortunately, about forty years after the work was created, the house in which it was displayed was destroyed

> *"What can be known about God is plain to them. . . . For [God's] invisible attributes, namely, his eternal power and divine nature, have been clearly perceived, ever since the creation of the world, in the things that have been made [poiema]."*
>
> **Romans 1:19–20**

> *"For we are his workmanship [poiema], created in Christ Jesus."*
>
> **Ephesians 2:10**

by an earthquake, smashing the oil-on-wood panel into seventeen separate pieces.

Another artist used long iron nails and blocks of wood to piece the fragments of the painting back together, and then painted over it to conceal the breaks. Over the years, so many layers of paint were added to cover the damage that the original colors were completely obscured.

In 1998, experts began what turned into a massive, ten-year restoration project aimed to return the painting to its original splendor. The laborious undertaking required a multidisciplinary team effort involving about fifty people,

including wood specialists and photography technicians. Painstaking labor was required to fix the shattered areas, remove layers of paint and dirt, and get the colors back to their magnificent hues.

The result is stunning. The cracks are gone. Centuries of brown film and grime are gone. The dulling veneers and patches have been stripped away. The finished product glows with the deep reds, blues, and golds of the original work. The restoration also revealed intricate details in the painting that had long been concealed, including several plants.

Given how badly it was damaged, the restoration of Raphael's painting is arguably even more amazing than the painting itself. The original was splendid. But the miracle of restoration enhances the beauty. Knowing the drama of the whole story, one can only gaze in wonder. The creation was great. But the re-creation is even greater.

The spiritual parallels are obvious and profound. No matter how greatly sin has damaged your life . . . no matter how many dull, ugly layers of paint and veneer you may have applied in an unsuccessful attempt to cover the cracks . . . no matter if the colors are faded or the picture is so obscured that you can barely see the original . . . God is in the restoration business. He is a great, redeeming God who is making all things new, through the work of Christ on our behalf. His divine power and love can re-create and restore your life to its original design—that beautiful work of art intended to display the loveliness of Christ!

Are you committed to having a makeover? Are you willing to obey "from the heart"? Will you let Him re-create you according to His divine design?

In the space below, write out a prayer asking the Lord to do a beautiful, complete work of restoration in your life.

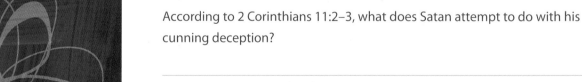

beautiful devotion

*"Thus says the LORD,
'I remember the
devotion of your youth,
your love as a bride,
how you followed me
in the wilderness,
in a land not sown.'"*

Jeremiah 2:2

*"For I feel a divine
jealousy for you, since
I betrothed you to one
husband, to present
you as a pure virgin to
Christ. But I am afraid
that as the serpent
deceived Eve by his
cunning, your thoughts
will be led astray from
a sincere and pure
devotion to Christ."*

2 Corinthians 11:2–3

At the beginning of the last century, a young woman named Amy Carmichael rescued a young Indian girl from being sold into prostitution. Over the next few years, she took in more and more girls destined for the same horrible fate. This led to the founding of Dohnavur Fellowship, an organization committed to the rescue, care, feeding, and education of hundreds of children.

The ministry grew rapidly. Desperate for help, Amy sent a letter to the pastors in the region, asking if they had any women *"wholly devoted to our Lord and separate in spirit from the world"* who would be free for this work. The pastors wrote back with essentially the same reply:

> *Not only have we no women like this, but we do not know of even one woman of the kind you want.*[1]

Between all the churches in the region, the pastors could not identify even one woman who was passionately and wholeheartedly devoted to the Lord.

Read the verses in the margin. What type of attitude does the Lord want His bride to have? (Hint: the word appears in both verses.)

_____

_____

According to 2 Corinthians 11:2–3, what does Satan attempt to do with his cunning deception?

_____

_____

The word "devotion" in Jeremiah 2:2 is translated from the Hebrew word *chesed*. *Chesed* is a powerful word that includes the ideas of covenant-keeping love, goodness, kindness, mercy, and faithfulness. It is often translated "steadfast love" in the Old Testament.

The English dictionary says that devotion means deep, steady affection, loyalty, and faithfulness. So the English word comes fairly close to conveying the right idea. But it doesn't fully capture the concept of devotion taking place in the context of a "covenant," which is a formal (legal) agreement solidifying a relationship.

According to 2 Corinthians 11:2–3, what type of covenant devotion ought we to display toward Christ?

- ☐ The devotion of a friend to a friend
- ☐ The devotion of a sister to a brother
- ☐ The devotion of a girlfriend to her boyfriend
- ☐ The devotion of a child to a parent
- ☐ The devotion of a bride to her groom

Among the Jews, betrothal was the first stage of marriage, similar, in some ways, to our modern-day concept of engagement. But unlike engagement, a Jewish betrothal was binding. It involved a formal marriage covenant in which the couple legally became husband and wife. The betrothal could only be canceled by the death of one or both partners.

Although they were legally married, the betrothed couple did not live together nor did they have sexual relations during the period of betrothal, which normally lasted about a year. At the end of that time, they went through a marriage ceremony. The marriage was blessed by family and friends and celebrated with a great feast. The couple then physically consummated the marriage and began to live together.

According to Paul, the church is betrothed to Jesus Christ. Because of the new covenant in His blood, we have legally become His bride. But we still await our formal "presentation" to Him, which will take place at the "marriage supper of the Lamb" (Rev. 19:7–9).

As a spiritual "father of the bride" (see 1 Cor. 4:15), Paul was concerned about guarding and protecting the purity of his "daughter" in Corinth. He wanted to make sure that her love, adoration, and commitment to her Husband did not diminish during the betrothal period. He intended to escort her to the wedding in a stunningly beautiful and spotless dress, and proudly present her to her strong, tenderhearted, love-smitten Groom.

What are some ways in which a bride might display her devotion to her groom?

demonstrable devotion

What would you think if you met an engaged woman who neglected her fiancé and didn't want to spend time with him? What if she was unfaithful and cheated on him? What if she forgot to prepare for her upcoming wedding? You'd conclude that she wasn't truly committed to the marriage, wouldn't you? Because that's not how an engaged woman is supposed to behave.

In a healthy relationship, an engaged woman is devoted to her fiancé. She's enthralled with him. She constantly thinks about him, and wants to please him. She focuses on getting ready for their wedding and their future together. And she doesn't consider dating other guys! True Womanhood means having this same type of bridelike devotion to Christ, our Betrothed.

What are some ways in which a woman might demonstrate a sincere and pure devotion to Christ?

How devoted a bride are you? Fill out the following devotion report card. In the column to the right of each statement, give yourself a grade ranging from **A** to **D** for how devoted you are to Christ.

NOTE: [A] is "wholly devoted," [B] "quite devoted," [C] "somewhat devoted," and [D] "not very devoted"	Grade	
Your devotion is sincere (wholehearted) and pure. It is unpolluted by other affections. (2 Cor. 11:2–3)		
You demonstrate your devotion by making yourself ready for your Groom. (Rev. 19:7–9)		
You demonstrate devotion by repenting of your sin and clothing yourself in righteous deeds. (Rev. 19:7–9)		
You demonstrate your devotion by cultivating godly character—by being pure, virtuous, self-controlled, gentle, kind, joyful, and so on. (Eph. 5:25–27)		
You demonstrate devotion by following your Groom's lead, even when it's difficult to do so. (Jer. 2:2)		
You are as loving and devoted as you were when your relationship first began. (Jer. 2:2; Rev. 2:4)		

Christ's rich, eternal commitment to us is the foundation and source of our devotion to Him. His love and grace make up for all the ways in which we fall short. Even if your report card was filled with Ds—or perhaps one or more Fs—Jesus' devotion to you does not change.

Just as an engaged woman eagerly, lovingly prepares for her wedding, desirous to be her most beautiful for her groom, so the thought of being eternally wedded to our holy Groom should motivate us to spend our lives here on earth wholly devoted to Him.

Before we close this lesson, if you're married, we want you to do one more exercise. Go back and fill out the shaded part of the report card. Give yourself a grade for how devoted you are to your husband. When you're done, come back and finish reading. . . .

How did you do? Here's the point we want you to take away from this: God created woman to display the "bride" part of Christ's redemptive story. That means a wife is supposed to relate to her husband in the same way the church is to relate to Christ. Of course, the correlation isn't exact, since Christ is without sin and husbands aren't. But the pattern is there nonetheless. Your devotion to your husband is one of the most powerful ways you can display your devotion to Christ.

→ **Close today's lesson in prayer**. Ask the Lord to deepen your devotion for Christ and, if you're married, for your husband.

beautiful character

> "So that he might present the church to himself in splendor, without spot or wrinkle or any such thing, that she might be holy and without blemish."
>
> **Ephesians 5:27**

> "Let us rejoice and exult and give him the glory, for the marriage of the Lamb has come, and his Bride has made herself ready; it was granted her to clothe herself with fine linen, bright and pure—for the fine linen is the righteous deeds of the saints."
>
> **Revelation 19:7–8**

A bride picking out a gown is always a momentous occasion. I (Mary) had the joy and privilege of joining my oldest son's bride-to-be, Jacqueline, along with her mother and father, as Jacqueline picked out a wedding dress in preparation for the big day. With the help of a bridal consultant, it wasn't long until she found "the dress." She looked stunning! It suited her perfectly. Beaming with the thrill of knowing how beautiful she was going to look for her groom, she eagerly said yes to the dress.

Months of planning and preparation culminated in that moment when the church doors opened and she stood dressed in her wedding gown, on the arm of her father, ready to be presented to her groom. Every bride is beautiful, but I can be a bit biased, can't I? I think Jacqueline was the most beautiful bride I have ever seen. Spotless, dressed in white, and radiant beyond all measure, she gracefully floated down the aisle.

I turned at that moment to watch my son, Clark, gaze at his approaching bride. I wanted to see "that look" . . . the one that was emblazoned in my memory almost thirty years ago, when I was the bride in white, walking down the aisle to meet my groom.

I can't fully describe the look. Its tenderness, joy, pride, purpose, longing, and fulfillment all mingled in one life-defining moment. It's the look that can only be seen in the eyes of a groom . . . and only at the moment when he is watching the fulfillment of his heart's desire draw near. I don't know why—maybe it's because I hear whispers of eternity calling—but it's always that breathtaking tender moment of a wedding that makes me cry.

As an earthly groom eagerly anticipates the moment when his bride walks down the aisle to meet him, beautifully arrayed in a spotless, white wedding dress, so the Lord Jesus anticipates the day when we will appear before Him, free from all defilement, clothed in His righteousness, to be His holy bride forever.

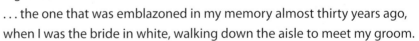

Read the verses in the margin on page 172. What does the splendid wedding attire of the church represent?

_____

_____

When the Bible talks about characteristics of the bride, it describes what the Lord wants for all of us. The directives include men—since they're part of the bride of Christ too. But it's particularly important for us women to listen up and pay attention to these passages, because "bride" is the part of the gospel story women are uniquely designed to tell. The spotlessness of the bride's wedding dress reflects the type of character that God desires for women. A True Woman is dressed in the beauty of holiness.

yes to the dress

*H*oliness and the adjective *holy* occur more than nine hundred times in the Bible. The primary Old Testament word for holiness means "to cut" or "to separate." It means "to be set apart, to be distinct, to be different." Holiness is a cutting off or separation from what is unclean, and a consecration or setting apart for that which is pure.

Holiness means setting aside our dirty, grubby clothes, and saying yes to the dress of righteousness that Christ has provided for His bride (Rev. 19:8). It also means clothing ourselves in godly character. Holiness isn't an abstract concept. It translates into practical, daily attitudes and behaviors.

Read Colossians 3:12–14. In the space below, list some of the aspects of godly character the Lord wants His bride to "put on" daily:

_____

_____

While all these traits of godly character are to be "put on" by both men and women, Scripture particularly emphasizes certain traits based on a person's age and gender.

Refer to Titus 2:2–6 to complete the following chart:

Character traits that Paul emphasizes for men:	Character traits that Paul emphasizes for women:

Paul urges older men to be sure that they are *sober-minded, dignified, self-controlled, sound in faith, sound in love*, and that they remain *steadfast*. Younger men especially need to work at developing *self-control*.

Older women are exhorted to be *reverent* (respectful). They are to avoid *slander* (control their mouths) and *much wine* (not to have self-indulgent, addictive habits). They are to train the young women *to love their husbands and children* (fondness/devotion to family), to be *self-controlled* (sensible) and *pure* (loyal/unadulterated/virtuous), to be *working at home* (managing their homes/welcoming and nurturing relationships), to be *kind* (gentle), and to be *submissive* to their husbands (amenable/deferring).

How do Paul's instructions to men counteract their sex-specific sin tendencies and point them back to their divine design?

_____

_____

How do Paul's instructions to women counteract our sex-specific sin tendencies and point us back to our divine design?

_____

_____

If Paul were to write you a personal letter, which of the character traits he identified as important for women would he encourage you to cultivate in a greater way in your life?

_____

_____

The nineteenth-century German philosopher Heinrich Heine said: "Show me your redeemed life and I might be inclined to believe in your Redeemer." [2] That's precisely Paul's point in Titus 2 and in the broader context of the entire epistle. Women (and men) whose character and behavior are in accordance with biblical teaching ("sound doctrine") point people to Christ and make the gospel visible and credible to believers and unbelievers alike.

As we are adorned with godly character, produced in us by the power of the Holy Spirit, we are preparing for That Day when we will "rejoice and exult and give him the glory" at the "marriage of the Lamb" (Rev. 19:7–8). The thought of seeing the joy in His eyes as He sees in the bride for whom He gave His life a pure reflection of Himself should motivate us to spend this life "making ourselves ready"—by His grace and the power of His Spirit—for that eternal union with our heavenly Bridegroom.

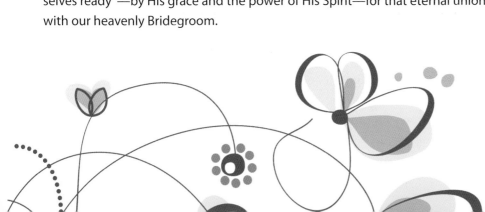

beautiful disposition

The feminist revolution was supposed to bring women greater fulfillment and freedom. But as women who have come to know and love God's original plan, we can't help feeling a sense of sadness over what has been forfeited in the midst of the upheaval —namely, the beauty, the wonder, and the treasure of the distinctive makeup of women. God created women to have a soft, beautiful, womanly disposition. But due to the distortions of sin and the flawed ideal for womanhood upheld by today's culture, most women have lost sight of who they were made to be.

Read 1 Peter 3:4–6 in your Bible. Describe the type of disposition that Peter associated with godly womanhood:

_____

_____

"But the meek [gentle] shall inherit the land and delight themselves in abundant peace."

Psalm 37:11

"The meek [gentle] shall obtain fresh joy in the LORD."

Isaiah 29:19

"Blessed are the meek [gentle], for they shall inherit the earth."

Matthew 5:5

Remember the metaphor of the Steel Magnolia? The image melds beauty with perseverance, softness with backbone, delicacy with durability, sweetness with stamina, and gentleness with gumption.

According to 1 Peter 3, the disposition of a truly beautiful woman is *gentle*, *quiet*, and *amenable* (that is, agreeable, submissive, honoring proper authority). That's the soft, delicate part.

At the same time, a True Woman is determined to do what's good and right and not give in to fear. She isn't swayed by popular opinion or intimidated by what others might say or do. That's the backbone-of-steel part. A godly woman's soft responsiveness is coupled with an uncompromising determination to respond appropriately—to say yes to the right things and no to the wrong things.

Our culture would have us believe that a soft womanly disposition is wimpy and repugnant—that we lose our personalities and personal identities and become weak, cowering doormats by embracing it. But a closer examination of the meaning of gentleness, quietness, and amenability demonstrates that this isn't the case at all. And as we begin to understand and live it out, the power and beauty of this womanly disposition becomes increasingly clear.

gentle disposition

G entleness (often translated "meekness") is a mild, friendly, considerate disposition. It's strength that accommodates to another person's weaknesses. In 1 Thessalonians 2:7, gentleness is portrayed as the type of disposition a nursing mother has as she cares for her fussy child. Though the baby may fuss, scream, and cry, she remains gentle in her response.

Gentleness is the opposite of being insistent on one's own rights, being rude or pushy, or demanding one's own way. It's the exact opposite of the "loud" attitude of the Wild Thing of Proverbs 7. Gentleness means we wholly rely on God rather than our own strength to defend ourselves against difficulty or injustice. It stems from trust in God's goodness and control over the situation. Gentleness isn't self-abasement. It's the mark of the wise woman who remains calm even in the face of other people's shortcomings.

Gentleness is "a tree of life" (Prov. 15:4). David noted that it was God's gentleness toward him that "made him great" (2 Sam. 22:36–37).

Read the verses in the margin on page 176. List some other benefits of a meek or gentle spirit. How do these benefits differ from what popular culture says women will get if they are meek?

_____

_____

When you encounter difficult or challenging situations, do you respond with "gentleness" or "loudness"? What do your responses reveal about your heart?

_____

_____

quiet disposition

A second aspect of a beautiful womanly disposition is "quietness." Again, this stands in marked contrast to the "loudness" that characterizes an ungodly woman (Prov. 7:11).

When we think of the word "quiet," the first thing we normally think of is audible sound or volume. We often equate "quiet" with "not talking." So does God expect us to shut our mouths and never say anything? Are we not allowed to express our opinions? Or discuss, deliberate, or disagree? Does godly womanhood mean we get out the duct tape and slap an "X" over our mouths? That we mutely nod our heads up and down like bobble-head dolls?

When the Bible talks about "quietness," it's not necessarily referring to an absence of talking. Although there's a connection, quietness has more to do

with the state of our hearts than the quantity and volume of our words. Even women who are outgoing, expressive, and sociable can exhibit a "quiet" spirit.

Quiet describes an attitude of calmness, serenity, and tranquility. It's being settled, steadfast, and peaceful. A quiet disposition is like a still, peaceful pool of water, as opposed to a churning, agitated whirlpool. A quiet spirit is the opposite of an anxious, distressed, disorderly, and clamorous one.

Quietness goes hand in hand with trust. "In quietness and in trust shall be your strength" (Isa. 30:15). Both are a result of righteousness: "the result of righteousness [is] quietness and trust forever" (32:17).

Read Isaiah 57:20–21 in the margin. What are some examples of "mire" and "dirt" that might be tossed up in relationships when a woman lacks a quiet spirit?

_____

_____

Explain how the state of a woman's spirit is connected to the quantity and quality of her words.

_____

_____

amenable disposition

A third aspect of a beautiful womanly disposition is the inclination to submit. We believe the Lord created women with a disposition—an inclination—to respond positively to being led. We are the responder-relators created with a "bent" to be amenable.

The word "amenable" comes from the French *amener* (to lead). As we learned earlier in this study, an ***amen***able woman says "Yes, Amen!" to input. She responds positively to guidance and direction. She welcomes it.

A godly woman is a "lead-able" woman. This stands in marked contrast to how an ungodly woman responds to leadership. Proverbs 7 describes the foolish woman as "wayward." The Hebrew word for wayward means "to be stubborn and rebellious." It reflects a defiant, self-willed, obstinate, "nobody-tells-me-what-to-do" frame of mind.

Amenability is a disposition or tendency to yield to others. It's an attitude that respects others and esteems God's proper lines of authority. A deferential woman gladly foregoes personal desires and preferences to honor God-ordained authority. Amenability is seen in a married woman's bent to follow and submit to her husband's lead. It's the disposition that would have made Eve beam with contentment and joy when Adam exercised authority and leadership in naming her.

Whether married or single, an amenable woman affirms and encourages godly qualities and initiative in men by being responsive rather than resistant in her interaction with them. Of course, we're not talking about being amenable or responsive to sin. But even while saying no to sin, we can have a spirit that is inclined to be responsive, yielding, and deferential.

Amenability is the heart attitude that caused Mary to respond to the angel's startling news of her pregnancy with "Behold, I am the servant of the Lord; let it be to me according to your word" (Luke 1:38). And it's the beautiful disposition that God desires each of His daughters to cultivate.

Which aspect of a womanly disposition do you find to be the most challenging: gentleness, quietness, or amenability? Why?

_____

_____

How can you grow in the trait you identified? (Hint: the Bible verses in the margins of this lesson will help you know how.)

_____

_____

"FOR THIS IS HOW THE HOLY WOMEN WHO HOPED IN GOD USED TO ADORN THEMSELVES, BY SUBMITTING TO THEIR OWN HUSBANDS, AS SARAH OBEYED ABRAHAM, CALLING HIM LORD. AND YOU ARE HER CHILDREN, IF YOU DO GOOD AND DO NOT FEAR ANYTHING THAT IS FRIGHTENING."

I Peter 3:5–6

beautiful display

> "Your adornment
> must not be merely
> external—braiding
> the hair, and wearing
> gold jewelry, or putting
> on dresses; but let it
> be the hidden person
> of the heart, with the
> imperishable qual-
> ity of a gentle and
> quiet spirit, which is
> precious in the sight
> of God. For in this way
> in former times the
> holy women also, who
> hoped in God, used to
> adorn themselves."
>
> **I Peter 3:3–5**
> **NASB**

> "Likewise also
> that women should
> adorn themselves in
> respectable apparel,
> with modesty and
> self-control, not with
> braided hair and
> gold or pearls or
> costly attire, but with
> what is proper for
> women who profess
> godliness—with
> good works."
>
> **I Timothy 2:9–10**

Today's women are pursuing beauty at any cost. That's the conclusion of a YWCA report on the consequences of America's beauty obsession on women and girls.[3] The report notes that American women now spend some $7 billion a year, or an average of about $100 per woman per month, on cosmetics and beauty products. Over five years, that adds up to nearly a full year of tuition and fees at a public college.

If a woman were to cut back the amount she spent on beauty products by half, and invest it into her retirement account for ten years, she could save up to $10,000. The money spent on cosmetic products per year doesn't even factor in cosmetic surgical procedures, of which there are over 10 million a year. The economics of the never-ending treadmill of the pursuit of beauty are staggering.

What should we make of this compulsive desire of women to be beautiful? Is the pursuit of beauty wrong? We're going to answer in a way that may surprise you: First, we would argue that the pursuit of beauty is good and right, and an integral part of our wiring, as women. God creates and appreciates beauty and He has created us to long for and appreciate it too. This is especially true in the context of marriage—the Song of Songs demonstrates that it is totally fitting for a husband to enjoy and extol his wife for her beauty.

Second, we would suggest that the problem is not that we value beauty too much but that we don't value it nearly enough. When we consider the jaw-dropping beauty portrayed for us and offered to us throughout Scripture, it would seem that our desire for beauty is not too strong but too weak.

We try to doll ourselves up with the earthly and superficial and temporal, while the supernatural and eternal is offered us. To cite a favorite C. S. Lewis analogy, we're "like an ignorant child who wants to go on making mud pies in a slum because he cannot imagine what is meant by the offer of a holiday at the sea. We are far too easily pleased!"[4]

It's like the story that Jesus told about the pearl of great price. When a man discovered it in a field, he sold everything he had to purchase that field. When the pearl of great price caught his eye, all his other treasures seemed worthless in comparison. He joyfully gave them up to get the treasure whose beauty and value surpassed them all.

But here's the thing. Had he not caught a glimpse of the surpassing beauty of the pearl, he wouldn't have been willing to part with his meager possessions. He couldn't give up what was lesser until he caught sight of the greater. The reason women are so obsessed with cosmetics, creams, diets, and tummy tucks is that they have an insufficient understanding of what true beauty is all about, and their hearts haven't been gripped by a more compelling, more beautiful vision.

Read 1 Peter 3:3–5 and 1 Timothy 2:9–11 on the previous page.

The word "adorn" (Greek *kosmeo*) can also be translated as "to decorate" or "to beautify." It means "to put in order, arrange, make ready." A godly woman adorns herself. She exerts effort to make herself beautiful.

Summarize how godly women beautify themselves:

_____

_____

A godly woman has been gripped with a more awesome vision of beauty than a woman who does not know God. The gospel has revolutionized her understanding of what true beauty is. She's caught a glimpse of Christ, and it's taken her breath away. Displaying *that* beauty has become more important and desirable to her than pursuing the fleeting beauty of the world. And even her desire for external beauty is rooted in a heart to display *His* beauty.

It's not that she doesn't pay attention to clothing, hair, and makeup. Those things aren't *un*important. They're just not *as* important. When it comes to beauty, she's far more focused on getting the kind that lasts. She listens to God's ideas about what it means to be a beautiful woman—and she allows Him to conform her life to His design.

From the time I (Nancy) was a little girl, I have always dreamed of one day being a "godly, old woman." (I've come to realize that the "old" part comes more easily than the "godly" part!) Have you ever seen the kind of woman I'm talking about? Have you noticed how lovely she is?

"And the king will desire your beauty. Since he is your lord, bow to him."

Psalm 45:11

"Hear, O daughter, and consider, and incline your ear: forget your people and your father's house, and the king will desire your beauty. Since he is your lord, bow to him. The people of Tyre will seek your favor with gifts, the richest of the people. All glorious is the princess in her chamber, with robes interwoven with gold. In many-colored robes she is led to the king, with her virgin companions following behind her. With joy and gladness they are led along as they enter the palace of the king."

Psalm 45:10–15

Her skin may be thin and wrinkled, but she is radiant. Her vision may be failing, but her eyes sparkle. Her body may be stooped, but her spirit is still vibrant. So full of life! So full of wisdom! So full of love! So beautiful!!

Of course, you don't just wake up one morning and discover that you have become a "godly, old woman." (I wish!) There's no miracle cream on the market that will produce that kind of beauty—any more than there is some "instant" means of attaining physical beauty. The cultivation of spiritual beauty requires consistent, Spirit-inspired, grace-enabled, Christ-trusting effort.

And it takes time. The beauty we see in a godly old woman is the fruit of years of faithful application of a spiritual beauty regimen—spending time with the Lord, submitting to His design for her life, allowing His Spirit to develop in her the character of Christ. Her beauty flows from the inside out.

Which type of beauty is most attractive to you? Be honest. For each pair of statements, put a check beside the one that seems more appealing.

☐ Getting a great hairstyle ☐ Getting a gentle and quiet spirit	☐ Prettying up my face ☐ Prettying up my heart
☐ Dressing in nice clothes ☐ Dressing in holiness	☐ Choosing the right accessories ☐ Choosing to respect and obey
☐ Showcasing my beauty ☐ Showcasing Christ's beauty	☐ Wanting to look good ☐ Wanting to be and do good
☐ Studying fashion magazines ☐ Studying God's Book of fashion	☐ Wanting a makeup artist to make me over ☐ Wanting the Holy Spirit to make me over

I (Nancy) have to admit that when I first read the statements above (written by Mary), I thought, *"Ouch!"* I was convicted that I often place a greater premium and priority on external beauty than on cultivating internal beauty of the heart.

When it comes down to it, a hard, loud, clamorous, demanding, mouthy, obstinate, brash, controlling woman is neither beautiful nor womanly—no matter how attractive her external appearance might be. But a woman whose beauty flows from the inside out—a woman who clothes herself in the beauty of holiness, and embraces God's divine design for womanhood . . . WOW! Though she may not have the face and figure of a model, she's exceedingly beautiful and precious in God's eyes.

True Womanhood—the womanhood commended in God's Word—is spectacularly beautiful; more beautiful than any perfectly proportioned airbrushed model in any fashion magazine. How can that be? Because True Women represent the bride of Christ and reflect the glory of God and the gospel of Jesus Christ—and there's nothing more beautiful than that. The King of the universe is enthralled by that kind of beauty (Ps. 45:11) and angels look longingly on the scene—amazed at the display of the gospel (1 Peter 1:12).

Psalm 45 is a song celebrating the marriage of a Hebrew king to a foreign princess. Many commentators believe it is also a messianic prophecy that points to an even greater relationship, the one between Christ the King and His church-bride.

Read Psalm 45:10–15 in the margin on page 182. What does Psalm 45:11 suggest about why you should pursue beauty, and how you should go about pursuing it?

_____

_____

The bride in this royal wedding song is described as "all-glorious." A bride makes herself as beautiful as she can for her bridegroom. Scripture uses this imagery to illustrate how we are to make ourselves beautiful for our King. The Lord wants us to clothe ourselves in fine, spotless garments of righteousness—in holy character and holy deeds (Rev. 19:7–8). He also wants His daughters to cultivate a womanly disposition. Unlike mere physical beauty that diminishes as we get older (try as we might to retain it!), according to 1 Peter 3:4, this inner beauty is "imperishable" ("unfading," NIV). It is this disposition that is "very precious" and attractive in His sight.

It's amazing to consider that God created manhood, womanhood, and marriage as object lessons to help reveal His character and His redemptive plan. He wrote that parable directly on human flesh—He inscribed the divine illustration directly on you, and on each of the millions and billions of women and men who have ever lived.

Our desire is that this stunning vision will captivate your heart. We pray that it attracts you so much, and that you prize it so highly, that you will devote your life to the pursuit of true spiritual beauty—at any cost, and above every other kind of beauty.

drawing it out, drawing it in . . .

total makeover

process

The video for Week Seven will help you process this week's lessons. You'll find this week's video, a downloadable outline, and many more resources at www.TrueWoman101.com/week7.

ponder

Think about the following questions. Discuss them with your friends, family, and/or small group:

1. Have you ever felt that True Womanhood fell into the same sort of category as getting your teeth drilled—the right thing to do, but somewhat unpleasant? How does the idea that womanhood is the "poem" of God challenge this conception?

2. What are some behaviors that would indicate that a woman is devoted to a particular guy? What are some behaviors that would indicate that she is devoted to Christ?

3. What are the specific character traits that Paul emphasized for women (see Titus 2:2–6)? How do these character traits counteract our sex-specific sin tendencies and point us back to our divine design?

4. What are some character traits that Paul emphasized for men? How do these character traits counteract their sex-specific sin tendencies and point them back to their divine design?

5. What are some common misconceptions or caricatures about what it means to be gentle, quiet, and/or amenable? Do you think true femininity requires some women to violate their personalities?

6. As you consider the various aspects of true beauty we have looked at this week, is there a particular aspect of your womanhood in which you sense a need for the Lord to give you a total makeover?

personalize:

Use the following lined page to journal. Write down what you learned this week. Record your thoughts, comments, favorite verse, or an impactful idea or quote. Compose a prayer, letter, or poem. Jot down notes from the video or your small group session. We've provided this space so that you can personalize this week's lessons in the way that will best help you apply them to your life.

personalize it

drawing it out,
drawing it in . . .

sisterhood is powerful

The year was 1966. Betty Friedan invited about two dozen women to her hotel room to strategize on how to launch a feminist movement. The tireless efforts of those few led to the rapid mobilization of many. Just four years later, twenty thousand women marched proudly down New York's Fifth Avenue, identifying themselves as part of the women's liberation movement. It was then that Friedan boldly declared that no man, woman, or child would escape the nature of their revolution. She was right. Now, half a century later, feminism has become the prevailing mind-set of the masses.

So how did it happen? How did the ideas of so few get such widespread acceptance? Feminists will tell you it's because "Sisterhood Is Powerful." Women have a tremendous capacity to influence. When they work together, they can become an indomitable force for change.

How a few resolute women caused such a profound change was one of the topics of discussion when I (Nancy) invited Mary and a couple of other friends over to my home after recording some radio programs for *Revive Our Hearts* in the fall of 2002. Mary's book *The Feminist Gospel* had helped me understand how the feminist movement had penetrated and permeated not only our culture but even our churches. So I wanted her to help our listeners grasp how we got where we are today.

The four of us sat around in my living room that evening. Perhaps it would be more accurate to say that three of us sat. I was struggling with a bad cold, so I was laid out on the sofa, wrapped in a fuzzy blanket, cradling a box of tissues, and feeling the effects of some strong cold medication!

And here's where I (Mary) pick up the story . . . . Holly Elliff, Kim Wagner, and I were sitting around Nancy's living room that night, having a lively discussion about feminist philosophy, the women's movement, the carnage feminist ideology had caused in women's lives, and various related topics. One of us had just marveled at how such a small group of radicals had spearheaded the change when a voice piped up from the cocooned lump on the sofa:

> *If a few angry, determined women made such a profound impact for evil, just think what kind of impact a few godly, determined women could make for good. I think it's time for a counterrevolution.*

Nancy's statement halted our conversation like a school crosswalk attendant halting rush-hour traffic. It was so true. But it was getting late—and none of us felt particularly determined. Not to mention that the person who had sounded the call to arms needed to go to bed and was in no shape to lead or mobilize a revolution. I had a plane to catch. And the others had dizzying to-do lists compiled for the next day.

We laugh about it now, but looking back, the Lord used that conversation to water seeds He had been planting in my heart and in Nancy's for several years. In more recent years, those seeds have continued to take root and have borne much fruit, including multiple True Woman national conferences, the True Woman Manifesto, and much of what God is doing through the True Woman movement today.

Nancy's words proved to be prophetic. It IS time for a counterrevolution. But not a strident political one. It's time for a quiet counterrevolution of godly men and women who dare take God at His Word, stand against the popular tide, and delight in His divine design for manhood and womanhood. And with the Lord, one can "chase a thousand, and two put ten thousand to flight" (Deut. 32:30 NASB)—few can impact many.

This revolution will not involve protests, sit-ins, marches, or media spectacles. It will not be underwritten by government funding. It will not need celebrity endorsement, swanky commercial marketing, or sophisticated ivory-tower polish. Nor will it clamor for acceptance in the public square.

It will be a grassroots movement of ordinary women who love Jesus, who aim to be fruitful, aim to be welcoming, aim to be helpful, aim to leave a legacy, and aim to make a difference. Sisterhood is powerful. Few will impact many, as woman after woman says "Yes, Lord!," embraces His beautiful design, and links arms and hearts with other like-minded women. →

aim to be fruitful

O Our society encourages women to pursue career, success, power, sex, and self-fulfillment as their ultimate aim. In the wake of the modern feminist revolution, marriage and motherhood have been severely devalued. Feminism claims that these institutions keep women in a state of servitude and prevent them from fulfilling their true potential. Children are seen as a burden or a limitation on women's happiness and their ability to make a mark on the world.

An early mantra of the feminist movement was that biology—a woman's ovaries, womb, and capacity to bear children—must not determine a woman's destiny. But according to Scripture, godly, intentional mothering is integral to womanhood. A woman's physical capacity to give birth points to our spiritual purpose and calling. Bearing and nurturing life is what God has "hardwired" women to do.

Every normal woman is equipped to be a mother. Certainly, not every woman in the world is destined to make use of her biological equipment. But motherhood, in a much deeper sense, is the essence of womanhood. The first woman's name affirms and celebrates this truth: Eve means "life-giver." God's purpose is that every woman—married or single, fertile or infertile—will bring forth life. Regardless of her marital status, occupation, or age, a woman's greatest aim ought to be to glorify God and further His kingdom by reproducing—bearing spiritual fruit.

Read the verses in the margin. According to 1 Timothy 5:10, what is one of the primary "good works" that God prepared for women?

_____

_____

From the beginning, it was God's intent that His people would "be fruitful and multiply and fill the earth" (Gen. 1:28; 9:1; 17:6; 35:11). But He didn't want women to simply bear children for the sake of increasing the

> *"For we are his workmanship, created in Christ Jesus for good works, which God prepared beforehand, that we should walk in them."*
>
> **Ephesians 2:10**
>
> *"And having a reputation for good works: if she has brought up children."*
>
> **1 Timothy 5:10**

human population—to be mindless, perpetual baby-making machines. No. He had something much more vital in mind. Women were an essential part of His strategic plan. He wanted us to be fruitful for the purpose of advancing and expanding the family of God (Gal. 3:7). The point of motherhood is to bring forth and nurture children in the faith. God blesses a woman with children so that she might expand His kingdom.

fruit for the kingdom

In this context, we need to understand that motherhood is a crucial part of God's redemptive plan. It's critical to preserving and passing on truth to the next generation. And because it's so important, there has always been an attempt on Satan's part to undermine it. Today there is an intense battle in this arena. On the one hand, society disdains and denigrates motherhood as an important part of womanhood. This thinking clearly is not in line with God's Word. On the other hand, there are some who promote the idea that bearing biological children is the end-all and be-all of womanhood. This thinking is also wrong, and in need of correction.

First, the Bible places a huge value on having and raising children. One of the great purposes of marriage is to bear and raise children for the glory of God. It is a high and holy calling to be a wife and a mother, and we need to become cheerleaders once again for women who embrace the mission of marriage and motherhood as a means of glorying God and advancing His kingdom. Throughout Scripture, we see that children are a blessing. God loves them! If you have a negative attitude toward children, then your heart is not in line with the heart of God.

Second, while marriage normally results in giving birth to biological children, this is not always the case, nor is it our ultimate goal. Woman's ultimate aim is to be spiritually fruitful—to bear and raise spiritual offspring. To the unmarried, Paul affirmed that singleness is a gift from God, and that "each has his own gift from God, one of one kind and one of another" (1 Cor. 7:7).

God gives us different gifts and callings. The gift of marriage is not given to every woman, nor is the gift of bearing children. It is not a given that every woman will marry, or that every married woman will be able to bear children, or that every woman ought to bear as many biological children as she possibly can. What IS a given is that *all* women are called to be spiritually fruitful. The

Lord wants all women—including single and childless women and women past childbearing age—to have a "household" and be the "joyful mother of children."

Read the verses in the margin. In Psalm 113:9, underline the word "household" and the phrase "joyful mother." How should this mind-set be reflected in our view of children? Explain how a childless woman might have a "household" and be the "joyful mother of children."

_____

_____

Remember Deborah in the book of Judges? We know that Deborah was married. The Scripture doesn't tell us how old she was or whether she had biological children. But it does tell us that Deborah saw herself as "a *mother in Israel*" (Judg. 5:7). She didn't describe herself as a ruler, judge, prophet, or leader . . . but as a *mother in Israel*. She had a God-given, protective, nurturing instinct that gave her courage and compassion. She was not driven by the things that drive many modern women—power, control, position, or recognition—but by a mother's heart. She used her position and influence to fulfill her calling to motherhood.

The apostle Paul illustrates this point in Romans 16:13. Paul greets his friend Rufus, and then passes on a greeting to Rufus's mother, "who has been a mother to me as well." We don't know anything else about this woman. We don't know whether she was still married or widowed—whether she traded merchandise like the Proverbs 31 woman, or financially supported Paul's ministry as Joanna and Susanna supported Christ's (Luke 8:1–3), or whether she mentored Paul in faith and doctrine as Lois and Eunice mentored Timothy (2 Tim. 1:5; 3:14). All we know is that she biologically and spiritually mothered Rufus, and that in some way, she also spiritually mothered Paul.

I (Mary) think of my own mother. She has six biological children (five brothers and me). But she has dozens and dozens more spiritual children. She is over eighty years old, and is still being fruitful and mothering. I think of my friend Joy Fagan, an unmarried woman who has been teaching at a Christian university for almost twenty years. She's much more than a professor to her students—she's a "mother" to them. Besides that, she's opening a halfway house to take in women released from the local prison and those escaping prostitution—she intends to "mother" them too, and to become a "grandma" by training her students to be spiritual moms.

I think of Anna, the college student who volunteers at the local crisis pregnancy center; and Jen, the accountant who helps struggling single moms do tax returns; and Meagan, who leads a small group Bible study for teen girls; and Janice the dentist who goes on mission trips to provide free dental care for the needy; and Wilma, a single woman who serves as the children's and women's ministry director at my church; and Carrie, the mom who leads a MOPS group at the local school; and Grace, who stays home and schools her kids. All these women—some with biological children and some without—are fulfilling their mission and calling to godly motherhood.

Though I (Nancy) have never been married and have not had the privilege of giving birth to physical children, God has given me countless opportunities to invest and nurture spiritual life in others—whether in my friends' children, in younger women He brings across my path, or in young married couples who have lived in my home over the years. What a joy it has been to receive notes like this one from a thirtysomething mom who calls me "Mama Nancy":

> I couldn't let this day go by without saying "Happy Mother's Day"! You have been like a "mother" to me in so many ways and for that I'm so thankful! I know I wouldn't be where I am today without your "laboring" of love, countless hours of studying His Word, taking precious time to teach what He would have you to. Thank you for continually saying yes to Him! Thank you for being my biggest cheerleader!

Read the verses in the margin. What is the ultimate aim of both biological and spiritual motherhood?

_____

_____

What opportunities has God placed in your current life situation to "joyfully mother children"?

_____

_____

→ **God has fashioned and equipped us as women to be "mothers,"** to bring forth godly fruit for His glory and for the advancement of His kingdom. There is no higher calling or more vital responsibility!

"WALK IN A MANNER WORTHY OF THE LORD, FULLY PLEASING TO HIM, BEARING FRUIT IN EVERY GOOD WORK AND INCREASING IN THE KNOWLEDGE OF GOD."
Colossians 1:10

"YOU . . . BELONG TO ANOTHER, TO HIM WHO HAS BEEN RAISED FROM THE DEAD, IN ORDER THAT WE MAY BEAR FRUIT FOR GOD."
Romans 7:4

aim to be welcoming

"I want younger women to marry, have children, manage their households, and give the adversary no opportunity to accuse us."

I Timothy 5:14
HCSB

"Train the young women to love their husbands and children, to be self-controlled, pure, working at home ..."

Titus 2:4–5

Revive Our Hearts hosts a number of websites, blogs, and Facebook pages, all designed to help women experience greater freedom, fullness, and fruitfulness in Christ.* Reading the comments readers post on these sites helps us keep a pulse on the thinking of Christian women. Many of the comments posted by teens—the women of the next generation—are particularly revealing, as they grapple with the call to embrace biblical womanhood and what that looks like. One gal said,

> *I don't really agree with all this. I'm not a helper —trust me. I just like never help, although I should more. I simply CAN'T cook. I hate cleaning. I'm very strong-willed, and I have a hard time submitting. . . . I'm not a real girly girl. I would rather play a good game of paintball than bake a cake! And I've like NEVER, EVER, EVER changed a single diaper in my life! And I'm really bad with babies! Trust me!!!*

> *I love school, so that's why I'm going to college when I graduate next year, and I'm going to get a job after that. To be honest, I don't even think that I want to have kids . . . I'm just not the serving, submitting, cooking, cleaning, baby, helping type, so I just don't fit into this model of the way femininity is supposed to look like! And so how am I supposed to be soooo feminine when I get married? Do I have to change who I am? 'Cause I'm NOT!*

Another said,

> *Why could [marriage] not include a woman with a career that satisfies her, and maybe even a man who is satisfied at home being a homemaker, rather than traditional male/female roles? I don't think that means you're not embracing your femininity but that you're embracing that which makes you happy.*

---

* We have three different blogs: the *True Woman* blog, the *Revive Our Hearts* blog, and the *Lies Young Women Believe* blog, which focuses on teenage girls. Mary also has a blog called *Girls Gone Wise*. We encourage you to visit these websites, where you can interact with other women, younger and older, who desire to be True Women of God.

These kinds of statements raise multiple concerns in our minds:

- These teens equate biblical womanhood with a stereotypical checklist of who does what around the house.

- They regard child care and domestic activities with disdain.

- They have swallowed culture's gender-neutral ideal and don't understand the innate differences between male and female.

- They believe a woman's satisfaction is more tied to her career than her relationships.

- They think biblical womanhood is unfulfilling—they suspect it might violate a woman's personality and potential.

- They think they have a better idea about what will make women happy than God does.

In today's lesson, we're going to look at some of these misconceptions head-on. One of God's beautiful purposes for the woman is that she creates and manages a welcoming home. As you'll soon see, He doesn't provide a specific checklist of chores she must do, nor does He specify that she is the one who must exclusively do them, nor does He expect that looking after the home will be the sum total of all a woman does (the Prov. 31 woman also ran a business), nor does He want her to obsessively idolize the home and value it above that to which it points.

But regardless of these common faulty caricatures and ideas about what it all entails, Scripture makes it clear that God did create women with a unique "bent" and responsibility for the home. Married or single, women can glorify God by creating warm, inviting spaces that are conducive to welcoming and nurturing life.

Read the verses in the margins of pages 192 and 194. Why do you think God assigned woman (and not man) the primary responsibility for creating and managing a home?

Do you feel that this assignment is demeaning to women? Explain.

_____

_____

According to 1 Timothy 5:14 and Titus 2:5, the responsibility for managing the home falls primarily (though not exclusively) on the woman's shoulders. The Greek word translated "working at home" in Titus 2:5 means to be busy at home, active in household duties; it means to be domestically inclined. Domesticity is an old-fashioned word we don't hear much about anymore. And if we do hear it, it's often not in a positive sense. Do you know what the word "domestic" means? The heart of domesticity is a devotion to home life. It's having a heart for the home.

In the space below, list some physical, emotional, and spiritual benefits an inviting home provides for those who live in it:

_____

_____

a taste of heaven

Did you know that Jesus is domestic? Does that sound strange to you? Why would we say that? Listen to these verses in John 14. Jesus said, "Let not your hearts be troubled. . . . In my Father's house are many rooms. . . . I go [*to do what?*] to prepare a place for you . . ." (vv. 1–2). What is Jesus doing right now? He's creating a peaceful, joyful home for us in His Father's house—a place where our hearts will never again be troubled. So as women, when we create welcoming homes where Christ is honored, we're creating here on this earth, a physical, visible reflection of an eternal, invisible reality. We're giving people a taste of heaven.

Here again, our womanhood displays and points to something far greater than ourselves.

This world is a messy, chaotic place. But we have the privilege of creating a home environment that makes people long for heaven. Whether married or single, our goal as women is to create a place, physically and spiritually, that beckons and welcomes people "home." A place that ministers to their

needs—where they can find comfort, healing, rest, love, and a sense of belonging. A peaceful nurturing place where they can retreat to renew their hearts and be untroubled. A place that gives them a sense for how wonderful our eternal home will be.

Both in the physical space and in the spiritual climate of our homes, the Lord wants us to create a place where family members long to come. And not just biological family. We can reflect the hospitable heart of God by opening our hearts and homes to those outside our family—even strangers. By practicing hospitality, we demonstrate in a visible, tangible way that His heavenly home is open to those who enter by faith.

How does the meaning and value that the Bible places on woman's domesticity differ from the meaning and value culture places on it?

_____

_____

How can a biblical perspective on the home help women avoid the trap of comparison or idolizing the pricey, pristine "Martha Stewart" image of home presented in women's magazines?

_____

_____

Does God's design for women to be welcoming keepers of the home call for any adjustments in your heart and/or habits? Explain.

_____

_____

aim to be helpful

The comment we looked at yesterday, posted by a teen on the *Lies Young Women Believe* blog, expresses a common sentiment. Feminism has convinced most of us that "serving, submitting, cooking, cleaning, babies, and helping" are demeaning, and trap women in a second-sex, subservient role. These are things to which few modern girls aspire.

> *I'm not a helper—trust me. I just like **never** help, although I should more. . . . I'm just not the serving, submitting, cooking, cleaning, baby, helping type.*

Sadly, what this girl is really acknowledging is that she doesn't value what God values. The things that are precious to Him are disdainful to her. Because Christ is definitely the serving, submitting, helping type! And He doesn't consider this to be a demeaning role (Phil. 2:6–8). You could even argue that Christ is also the cooking, cleaning, baby type. It was His submissive obedience to the Father that cooks up the ingredients of redemption, cleans us up, and produces spiritual babies for the family of God.

When we think of the word *helper*, we normally think of a role that's secondary to another, more vital role. There's the plumber, and then there's the plumber's *helper*. The plumber is the important one. He's the go-to guy with all the know-how and experience. The helper is dispensable—nice to have around, but not critical to getting the job done. The helper gets bossed around by the plumber. The helper does all the stuff the plumber doesn't want to do. The plumber fits the pipes together, saves the day, and collects the big paycheck. But the helper gets no glory

and no recognition. The helper only exists to make the plumber's life easier and to clean up his mess.

Though this is a common view with regard to the value and role of a helper, it's not at all in line with the biblical meaning of the word.

"Then the LORD God said, 'It is not good that the man should be alone; I will make him a helper fit for him.'"

Genesis 2:18

The concept of being a "helper" is used of all three members of the Godhead. The Father is our helper (Ps. 54:4); Christ helps His people (Heb. 2:16); and the Holy Spirit is our helper (John 14:16). Elsewhere, the term is used of military and political allies (1 Chron. 12:18; Jer. 47:4; Nah. 3:9). So the idea of a lesser position or status is entirely absent from the biblical definition of the word.

Nor does the word imply that the helper is stronger than the one being helped—though God is clearly stronger than we are. The word simply indicates that those in need of a helper's assistance do not have enough to get the job done on their own. Their resources are inadequate for the task. A "helper" provides something that the person in need of help does not have.

Read Genesis 2:18 in the margin on page 196. Based on the biblical meaning of the word "helper," explain how woman is a helper fit for man.

Earlier in this study, we saw that God created woman to be a *helper fit for* man. The phrase translated "fit for him" means suitable, comparable, matching, or corresponding. It could literally be interpreted as, "like opposite him."[1] The woman was "tailor-made" for the man. What she brings to the table perfectly complements what he brings to the table. Both contribute something that's essential to getting the job done. The word *fit* stresses that, unlike the animals, woman is man's equal and can truly be one with man (Gen. 2:24) in his quest to glorify God. She enjoys full fellowship and partnership in humanity's God-given task of rule and dominion (1:27–28).

How would you explain to someone that woman's design to be a helper to man is a high, noble calling, rather than a demeaning or inferior role?

A helper is the opposite of a hinderer. It's fascinating to do a survey of Scripture to get a better grasp of what being a helper is about.

The following chart lists some traits of a helper. Complete the chart by identifying the opposite trait—that of a hinderer. The first one is done for you.

HELPER	HINDERER
Is near (Ps. 22:11)	Is aloof, antagonistic
Notices and cares (Pss. 10:14; 40:17)	
Comes quickly to aid (Ps. 22:19)	
Comforts (Ps. 86:17)	
Heals (Ps. 30:2)	
Never casts off or forsakes (Ps. 27:9)	
Strengthens, upholds, supports (Isa. 41:10; Ps. 20:2)	
Keeps from falling (Ps. 118:13)	
Counsels and declares sound knowledge (Job 26:2–4)	
Builds confidence (Ps. 118:7)	
Combats fear (Heb. 13:6)	
Promotes order and security (2 Sam. 23:5)	
Fights adversity alongside (2 Chron. 32:8)	
Encourages and gladdens (Ps. 33:20–21)	

Being a "helper" is a fundamental aspect of our design as women. This calling certainly applies to a woman's relationship with her husband. But we believe it also extends beyond the marriage relationship. There are many ways we as women can help, rather than hinder, the men around us. We can help them:

- Glorify God (Isa. 43:7; Rom. 15:5; 1 Cor. 10:31)

- Exercise dominion and stewardship over the earth (Gen. 1:28; Ps. 8:6)

- Be spiritually fruitful and multiply (Gen. 1:28; Rom. 9:8) and do good works for the kingdom of God (Eph. 2:10)

- Honor God through the testimony of sexual purity (1 Thess. 4:5–9)

- Embody and testify to the enormous grace of a breathtaking God (Rom. 1:17–23; Eph. 2:8; John 1:16)

 Women were designed to help men serve God's redemptive purposes in this world. That doesn't mean that every man needs a wife or every woman needs a husband. But it does mean that in the grand scheme of things, both sexes are necessary to accomplish what God wants humans to accomplish. Men cannot do it alone. A biblical view of the role of helper lifts womanhood out of the romance novel and power-puff gutter and gives it cosmic dignity, meaning, and purpose. And it helps us understand the value of tasks that our culture views as trivial or inconsequential.

There may be times in a woman's life when helping involves a seemingly endless list of chores like cooking, cleaning, and caring for babies in one season and for elderly parents in another. But we are never more like Jesus than when we are helping and serving others. And if a woman's help results in God's ultimate purposes being fulfilled, her work is vital, no matter how "small" the task may be.

Review the chart on page 198. Are you a helper or hinderer? Are there any ways you may be hindering the men around you from becoming all God created them to be?

aim to leave a legacy

S "Something is very wrong with the way American women are trying to live their lives today," Betty Friedan mused in 1963.[2] She proposed that women would not be happy—and the problem would not be solved—until women stopped serving the needs of the family, claimed the power to self-define, self-actualized themselves in the workforce, and neutralized the meaning of gender. Friedan's vision for womanhood became the legacy that her generation passed on to the women of this generation.

Looking back, it's obvious that the "Leave It to Beaver" model of womanhood—having a husband, a station wagon full of kids, a house in the 'burbs, and every possible modern appliance—didn't bring women the happiness they desired. In the throes of the early feminist movement in the early 70s, a *Time* magazine article lamented,

> *By all rights, the American woman today should be the happiest in history. She is healthier than U.S. women have ever been, better educated, more affluent, better dressed, more comfortable, wooed by advertisers, pampered by gadgets. But there is a worm in the apple. She is restless in her familiar familial role, no longer quite content with the homemaker-wife-mother part in which her society has cast her.*[3]

As we saw earlier, studies done in recent years show that women are even less happy today than they were back in the early years of the feminist revolution.[4] Clearly, all the "gains" of the women's movement have not produced the results they promised when it comes to women feeling more fulfilled or content.

Does that mean we ought to rewind the tape and try to squeeze every woman back into some 1950s—or perhaps 19th century, or earlier—mold? No. History proves that happiness

cannot be found in pursuing any cultural ideal. We can't hope to get womanhood right until we understand the ultimate object to which it points. Time, culture, and circumstances change, but the Bible provides an enduring model for womanhood that goes far beyond a stereotyped, cookie-cutter list of behaviors.

Sadly, for the most part, that model has been neglected and rejected in our day. And both we and our daughters are paying the price. Susan Hunt urges us to be resolute about recovering and passing on the legacy of biblically grounded, Christ-centered womanhood:

> We must recapture the legacy of biblical womanhood and carefully and intentionally pass it to the next generation. If one generation is careless, the next generation suffers. Relinquishing God's design for womanhood has devastating effects on the home, church, and culture.

> This battle for biblical womanhood is nothing new. It is simply the reclaiming of what always has been and always will be. But reclaim we must—for the glory of our sovereign King and the advancement of His kingdom.[5]

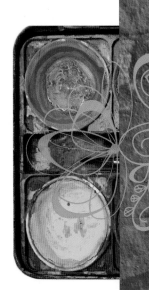

She's right. We believe it is worth the effort to preserve and promote God's pattern for our womanhood and to pass it on to those who are coming up behind us. If we fail to do so, successive generations will suffer.

In this study, we've tried to provide a vision of womanhood that transcends time and culture. We haven't given you a checklist of behaviors or emphasized the specifics of what true womanhood might look like in your life. For unless you understand the cosmic meaning of womanhood, and the principles that are to guide a woman's choices, you have little hope of making the right ones.

If the vision for womanhood you pass on to your daughters consists of a prescribed list of behaviors—issued at a particular point in time, for a particular cultural context—your daughter will be ill-equipped to figure out how to be a godly woman in her culture. And the legacy of true, biblical womanhood will once more be lost.

Read Psalm 78:1–8 in your Bible. Summarize why it's important to leave a legacy of True Womanhood for the daughters of the next generation:

_____

_____

_____

What are some possible effects of ignoring or rejecting God's design for womanhood—on women, the home, the church, and the culture?

_____

_____

_____

The beauty and enduring influence of a woman who embraces her divine design is a wonder to behold. One of my (Nancy's) dearest friends went home to be with the Lord in 2005, at the age of ninety-two. I knew Joyce Johnson as "Mom J," having lived with her and "Dad J" during my last two years of college. Though she was not a public figure, she was one of my heroes and left an indelible mark on my life. Her life was transformed and directed by the Word of God, rather than being conformed to this world.

Mom J faithfully loved and supported her husband through sixty-four years of marriage, until his death fifteen months before her own. She loved, served, and invested in the lives of her five children, seven grandchildren, and one great grandchild.

She had a servant's heart. There is no telling how many guests she hosted in her home, how many meals she served, how many loads of laundry she ran for her husband, children, and others. Her greatest longing was that each of her children and grandchildren would have a personal, vital relationship with Christ, and she prayed earnestly and persistently toward that end.

The last time we met, within weeks of her home-going, she told me excitedly, "I'm still mentoring a young woman!" *At ninety-two!* Several years before her death, when her church asked for older women who were willing to invest in the lives of younger women, Mom J volunteered and was paired with a single gal in her twenties. I had the joy of meeting that young woman at Mom J's memorial service. Only the Lord knows how long-lasting and far-reaching will be the ripple effects and legacy of just that one consecrated life!

The Bible presents a model for how the legacy of True Womanhood ought to be passed down from generation to generation. According to Titus 2:3–5, how do younger women learn what True Womanhood is all about?

_____

_____

If women fail to be intentional about modeling godliness and leaving a godly legacy, the "word of God may . . . be reviled." What might that look like?

_____

_____

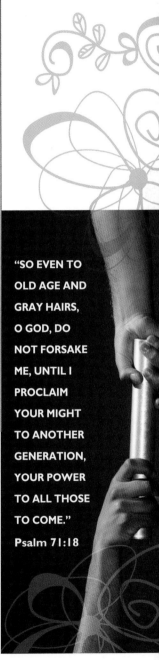

"SO EVEN TO OLD AGE AND GRAY HAIRS, O GOD, DO NOT FORSAKE ME, UNTIL I PROCLAIM YOUR MIGHT TO ANOTHER GENERATION, YOUR POWER TO ALL THOSE TO COME."
Psalm 71:18

The biblical pattern for womanhood involves passing the baton of faith to the next generation. It requires that we first *model* what it means for women to be filled with the Spirit and to live in accordance with sound doctrine (Titus 2:1). It also requires that we proactively *teach* the upcoming generation what True Womanhood is all about, and how to live lives that reflect the gospel of Christ.

The picture in Titus 2 is one of older women spiritually mothering younger women. Susan Hunt explains that spiritual mothering is simply "when a woman possessing faith and spiritual maturity enters into a nurturing relationship with a younger woman in order to encourage and equip her to live for God's glory."[6] According to this passage, spiritual mothering is not just a "nice idea" or an option; it is a mandate—and a high and holy privilege—for *every* Christian woman.

→ **How well are you fulfilling your mission to "pass the baton" on to the next generation?** Stop and ask the Lord if there are any further ways He may want you to be investing in the lives of younger women. Write down anything He puts on your heart.

_____

_____

aim to make a difference

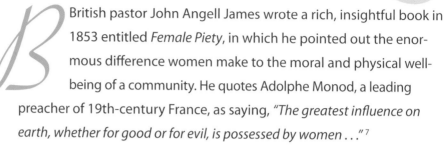

British pastor John Angell James wrote a rich, insightful book in 1853 entitled *Female Piety*, in which he pointed out the enormous difference women make to the moral and physical well-being of a community. He quotes Adolphe Monod, a leading preacher of 19th-century France, as saying, *"The greatest influence on earth, whether for good or for evil, is possessed by women . . ."* [7]

James believed that true womanhood was so vital that the strength and success of a nation depended on it. Without godly womanly influence, its moral fabric would unravel, families would fail, and it would certainly sink into degradation and ruin. He recognized the influence—for better or worse—that is exercised by every woman:

Every woman whether rich or poor, married or single, has a circle of influence within which, according to her character, she is exerting a certain amount of power for good or harm. Every woman, by her virtue or her vice, by her folly or her wisdom, by her levity or her dignity, is adding something to our national elevation or degradation . . .

A community is not likely to be overthrown where woman fulfills her mission, for by the power of her noble heart over the hearts of others, she will raise that community from its ruins and restore it again to prosperity and joy. [8]

It's true that each one of us as women has a sphere of influence within which we exert "a certain amount of power for good or harm." Sisterhood is indeed powerful. Our culture witnessed this firsthand in the past century, through the impact of the women's movement.

We believe it is time for a different kind of a women's movement—a quiet countercultural revolution of those who stand against the tide of culture and dare to delight in God's design. Our prayer is that by the power of His Spirit, godly women will ward off the destruction of gender, sexuality, male-female

relationships, morality, marriage, and family, and will use their influence to impact their communities for good and for godliness. Only God knows how great will be the ripple effect of that influence—for generations to come.

We want to wrap up this week by challenging you to step up and make a difference. It's our hope that you won't just finish this study and leave it at that. We pray that you will take things a step further by getting involved and intentionally helping to further this quiet counterrevolution.

make it a movement

In the 1970s, there was an advertising campaign that featured commercials with a young woman who cheerfully chirped that she "*told two friends about Faberge Organics Shampoo, who told two friends, who told two friends, and so on, and so on . . .*" while her image multiplied over and over again on the screen.

The potential of exponentially spreading a message by word-of-mouth is amazing. We did the math: if you tell two friends each week, who in turn tell two friends each week, then the message will spread to over half a million people in three months!

If every woman who does this study invites two other women to do it, and they invite their friends to do it, and we all begin to live out the call to True Womanhood, by God's grace, we could be used to turn the tide and make a profound difference in the lives of the next generation.

The goal of the True Woman movement is to help women:

- *Discover and embrace* God's design and mission for their lives

- *Reflect the beauty* and heart of Jesus Christ to their world

- *Intentionally pass* on the baton of Truth to the next generation

- *Pray earnestly* for an outpouring of God's Spirit in their families, churches, nation, and world

If that sounds like something you'd like to be a part of—or even if you're just curious to learn more—we encourage you to take the next step, and consider what you can do to get involved.

W We hope you'll spend more time hearing the heartbeat of the True Woman movement by visiting us online at www.TrueWoman101.com/ GetInvolved. You'll find links there to many helpful resources. For starters:

- Download the **videos** that accompany *True Woman 101*, as well as other related videos

- Follow the **True Woman Blog** (a great way to interact with other women on a daily basis)

- Take the **30-Day True Woman Makeover** (tens of thousands of women have been impacted by this exercise)

- Follow us on **Facebook** and **Twitter** (stay connected)

Here are ten additional ways you can get involved and make a difference:

1. **Sign the True Woman Manifesto**—We're trying to get 100,000 women to join us in a personal and corporate declaration of belief about what the Bible teaches about womanhood. You'll find a copy of the Manifesto beginning on page 214 in this study. If it expresses your heart, we'd encourage you to go online and sign your name to it. There's a video on the website explaining why we've put it together and why we think it's important for women to sign.

2. **Share the manifesto with your friends**—There's an online form that you can fill out to let your friends know that you've signed the True Woman Manifesto, and to encourage them to become part of this movement and sign it too. Remember, if every woman tells two friends who each tell two friends, the message will exponentially spread.

3. **Host a True Woman 101 Bible study**—Now that you've done this Bible study, you can do it again, with one or more of your sisters, daughters, coworkers, neighbors, relatives, and friends. There's plenty of help available. You can download a leader's guide, small group ideas, videos, handouts, and other resources at www.TW101.com.

4. **Host your own Girls-Night-Out or True Woman event**—Everything you need to pull off an effective True Woman event is on the website. You'll find schedules, event resources, a marketing pack, downloads, links to videos, a heart preparation guide, a manifesto signing ceremony, and all sorts of other goodies to help you get your friends involved in the True Woman movement.

5. **Recommend True Woman to your Facebook friends**—*"And she told two friends, and she told two friends, and so on, and so on. . . ."* You've got more than two friends on Facebook, don't you? So what are you waiting for? Recommend True Woman to your friends.

6. **Tweet and retweet about True Woman**—Our hash mark is #TrueWoman. You can help raise the profile of the True Woman movement by tweeting that you completed this study, tweeting that you're reading a True Woman book or attending a True Woman study, retweeting a True Woman blog post, or just telling the Twitter world how much of a difference True Woman has made in your life. Tweet. Tweet. You get the picture!

7. **Gift a True Woman book to a friend**—We have lots of recommended resources available in our online store. Purchase a book for a friend to help her learn about True Womanhood.

8. **Make a donation**—Every dollar counts. Your donation helps keep the website, the blog, and True Woman conferences going.

9. **Attend a True Woman conference**—Check out the schedule for the next True Woman conference. Plan to attend, and encourage your friends to attend. You could also plan to volunteer.

10. **Do another Bible study or book study about True Womanhood**— You could study:

    - *Girls Gone Wise—in a World Gone Wild* by Mary Kassian

    - *Lies Women Believe* by Nancy Leigh DeMoss

    - *Lies Young Women Believe* by Nancy Leigh DeMoss and Dannah Gresh

    - *Radical Womanhood* by Carolyn McCulley

We hope to develop additional Bible studies in the True Woman Curriculum Series. Watch for the release of True Woman 201 and 301.

Did you see something on the list that you could do to engage in the True Woman movement? Ask the Lord to direct your steps and show you specific ways you can get involved in this season.

becoming God's true woman

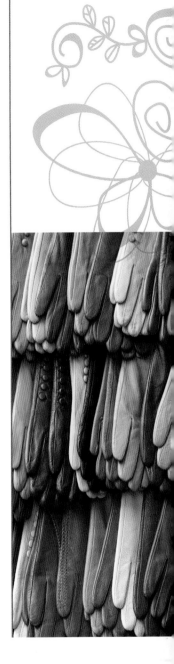

We hope this study has made a difference in your life. We challenge you to continue on the journey toward True Womanhood. But more than that, we challenge you to continue to get to know the One to whom the story of True Womanhood points—our Savior and friend, Jesus Christ. It's in saying yes to Him that your womanhood will be transformed to God's divine design.

drawing it out,
drawing it in...

sisterhood is powerful

process

The video for Week Eight will help you process this week's lessons. You'll find this week's video, a downloadable outline, and many more resources at www.TrueWoman101.com/week8.

ponder

Think about the following questions. Discuss them with your friends, family, and/or small group:

1. What does culture uphold as the ultimate aim of womanhood? How does it devalue marriage and motherhood?

2. In what sense is motherhood at the heart of womanhood? What are some of the implications of the saying that "The hand that rocks the cradle rules the world"?

3. Explain how a childless woman might have a "household" and be the "joyful mother of children" (Ps. 113:9 HCSB).

4. Why do you think God assigned woman the primary responsibility for creating and managing a home? How do you feel about this assignment?

5. How does the meaning and value that the Bible places on woman's domesticity differ from the meaning and value culture places on it?

6. What are some common misconceptions about the role of "helper"? In your relationships with men, would you categorize yourself as a helper or hinderer?

7. Why is it important to leave a legacy of True Womanhood for the daughters of the next generation?

8. What do you intend to do to support the vision for the quiet "counterrevolution" that we've shared?

personalize

Use the following lined page to journal. Write down what you learned this week. Record your thoughts, comments, favorite verse, or an impactful idea or quote. Compose a prayer, letter, or poem. Jot down notes from the video or your small group session. We've provided this space so that you can personalize this week's lessons in the way that will best help you apply them to your life.

personalize it

drawing it out,
drawing it in . . .

afterword: different by design

We hope this study has helped you understand more about your mission and calling as a woman. As we said at the outset, our intention has been to present timeless biblical principles that would apply to women of all cultures, personalities, ages, and stages of life. God created women with a divine design that differs from men. But He also created us different from one another. We are different by design.

throw away the cookie cutter

The Bible doesn't give us a simplistic, prescribed set of rules about what womanhood must "look" like. It doesn't tell us, for example, how long our skirts should be, or whether we should pursue advanced education, or that women must be the ones who clean the toilets and cook all the meals, or that we should never work outside of the home, or that all women should get married, or that we must educate our children a certain way. The Bible doesn't contain such checklists.

 Women are not the same. Womanhood will look different from woman to woman. It looks different for Mary than it does for Nancy. It may look different for your friend than it does for you. It may look different in Nigeria than it does in Canada . . . for a married woman than a single one . . . for a twenty-year-old than a sixty-year-old . . . for a gregarious woman than a quiet, reserved one . . . for an athlete than an artist . . . for an outdoorsy type than an indoorsy type . . . You get the idea!

That's not to say that our decisions don't matter. In His Word God has given us timeless principles about womanhood that transcend culture. It's important that we wrestle with how to implement these principles. We need to rely on the Holy Spirit's guidance to help us figure out how to apply them in our particular situation. But we must avoid a cookie-cutter mentality. We are all unique. Every woman's circumstances are distinct. We each need to carefully discern how to apply God's principles in our own lives, and we can encourage one another in that process; but it's not up to us to determine how they must be applied in other women's lives.

delight in the differences

We encourage you to delight in the diversity and to avoid the temptation to compare yourself with others. Cling firmly to core biblical convictions; hold less tightly to matters of application and preference. In both, be gracious and humble. Allow God to express His many-splendored grace through the various gifts and sensitivities He has given to different women who love Him and desire to honor Him.

It's also important to remember that True Womanhood is a journey. It certainly has been for both of us. The Lord has challenged and changed our thinking and behavior over time. We are at a different place in our understanding and application of True Womanhood now than we were twenty or thirty years ago.

Furthermore, it's important to know that though we aim for the ideal, we live in a less-than-ideal world. Because of the reality of sin, experiencing and expressing the biblical ideal for womanhood will be exceptionally difficult in some circumstances. We are sinners. Men are sinners. God's grace can enable us to walk with Him and please Him in every situation, but great wisdom is needed to discern how to reflect God's heart and ways in a broken world.

True Women are not haughty, self-righteous, or condemning. They are encouragers rather than critics. They know they are hopeless and helpless apart from God's grace. And they are generous in giving grace to others. They extend grace to those who do not have the same convictions about what the Bible teaches about womanhood. They extend grace to those who make alternate decisions about how to apply biblical principles. They extend grace to those who are at a different stage of their journey. They extend grace to those who are dealing with tragic, formidable circumstances. They extend to others the same kind of grace they themselves have received from God.

beware of the dangers

Womanhood is a topic that impacts each one of us on a personal level. At times, that makes it a difficult topic to address and discuss. Many stereotypes, caricatures, and misconceptions exist. And some people use the Bible to defend views and practices that are anything but biblical. A woman who has been subjected to flawed instruction, examples, and experiences may be more resistant and defensive about the topic than someone who has not.

We have found that the assault on the biblical pattern for gender comes from both sides. It comes on the left, from those who would throw off all distinctions between male and female, deride God's pattern, and seek an egalitarian, gender-neutral type of existence. But it also comes on the right, from those who regard women as inferior, who demean, degrade, and assault them, or who insist on a stringent, legalistic, oppressive application of gender roles. It is therefore necessary to engage the battle on both fronts and to strive for a biblical perspective that avoids both extremes.

In this study, we've focused on role differences. We believe that in this culture, it's vital to understand and celebrate the differences between male and female. However, it's also vital that we not lose sight of all that men and women have in common. Christians need to uphold the value, dignity, and honor of women. Women are co-bearers of the image of God. We are heirs together with men. We have been granted co-dominion over the earth. Our differences ought to enhance and not detract from the mutuality and interdependence of the sexes. They should increase our appreciation and respect for one another, and contribute to unity and partnership.

marvel at the meaning

In closing, we want to remind you that as important as gender is, it's not nearly as important as that to which it points. True Womanhood is not an end in and of itself. Manhood, womanhood, marriage, and sex exist to put the story of Jesus Christ on display. Their purpose is to draw attention to the beauty and wonder of the gospel.

There's nothing quite as compelling as a really good romance, is there? We're all familiar with the story line. The dashing hero fights to rescue the lovely princess from evil. She falls head-over-heels in love with him. He proposes. Then they ride off into the sunset to live happily ever after.

Have you ever wondered why so many stories follow this basic plot? Or why participating in a real-life version is the dream of so many women? It's not because Hollywood came up with such a fantastic script, or because movie stars make romance so attractive. No. It's because God wanted people to know and participate in the

greatest love story of all time—the amazing, pursuing love of Christ for undeserving sinners.

Great romance stories merely hint at the love relationship between Jesus Christ and His bride. Earthly romances are to the Cosmic One like sparkling reflections of light dancing on water are to the blazing sun. They are not the fiery light. They only reflect fleeting glimmers of it.[1]

Our Father God created male and female, sex and marriage, to give us a physical picture of what a spiritual relationship with Jesus is all about. Jesus Christ, the sinless Son of God, came to earth to rescue His bride (the church) from the terrible consequence of sin—separation from God, spiritual and physical death. Christ loved His bride so much that He died on the cross to bear the punishment of sin in her place. He rescued her from evil and made a covenant commitment to her. In response to His initiative, she cannot help but love Him and has responded favorably to His proposal.

Spiritually, she is betrothed (engaged) to Him. She keeps herself for Him and readies herself for the day they will be forever united. It's a love story like no other. It's the story of the gospel. Christ's story is the story that earthly romance was created to tell.

We trust that by God's grace you have become a part of that great story. The fact is, it's impossible to be a True Woman apart from having a personal relationship with Christ and having His Spirit living within you. Apart from Him, you may strive and struggle to perform or to gain His favor; you may be able to conform to some external standard or to impress others with how "good" you are—but you will never have the grace and the power you need to be the woman He designed you to be, from the inside out.

We hope you've responded to Jesus' call, that you have repented of running your own life and going your own way, and that you have accepted His free gift of forgiveness and salvation. If you haven't, you can do that right now by praying and telling the Lord that you recognize His right to rule in your life, that you are turning to Him from your sin and rebellion against Him, that you receive by faith the death He died in your place on the cross, and that you want to enter into an eternal relationship with Him.

In the end, saying yes to Jesus is what True Womanhood is all about. We hope this study has inspired you to marvel, embrace, and delight in God's spectacular plan, and that you've begun to discover the beauty, joy, and fulfillment of being exactly who He created you to be. He wants you to be so much more than what the world upholds as the ideal. He wants you to be a True Woman!—a woman who says "Yes, Lord!"; a woman who by His grace patterns your life according to His *divine design*.

"The True Woman Movement is helping women understand that their value, their worth, their purpose, their definition, and their future are all bound up in the person of Jesus Christ." —JANET PARSHALL

True Woman Manifesto

*A personal and corporate declaration of belief,
consecration, and prayerful intent—
to the end that Christ may be exalted
and the glory and redeeming love of God
may be displayed throughout the whole earth*

SCHAUMBURG, IL
OCTOBER 11, 2008

We believe that God is the sovereign Lord of the universe and the Creator of life, and that all created things exist for His pleasure and to bring Him glory. [1]

We believe that the creation of humanity as male and female was a purposeful and magnificent part of God's wise plan, and that men and women were designed to reflect the image of God in complementary and distinct ways. [2]

We believe that sin has separated every human being from God and made us incapable of reflecting His image as we were created to do. Our only hope of restoration and salvation is found in repenting of our sin and trusting in Christ who lived a sinless life, died in our place, and was raised from the dead. [3]

We realize that we live in a culture that does not recognize God's right to rule, does not accept Scripture as the pattern for life, and is experiencing the consequences of abandoning God's design for men and women. [4]

We believe that Christ is redeeming this sinful world and making all things new, and that His followers are called to share in His redemptive purposes as they seek, by God's empowerment, to transform every aspect of human life that has been marred and ruined by sin. [5]

As Christian women, *we desire to honor God* by living countercultural lives that reflect the beauty of Christ and His gospel to our world.

To that end, we affirm that . . .

Scripture is God's authoritative means of instructing us in His ways and it reveals His holy pattern for our womanhood, our character, our priorities, and our various roles, responsibilities, and relationships. [6]

We glorify God and experience His blessing when we accept and joyfully embrace His created design, function, and order for our lives. [7]

As redeemed sinners, we cannot live out the beauty of biblical womanhood apart from the sanctifying work of the gospel and the power of the indwelling Holy Spirit. [8]

Men and women are both created in the image of God and are equal in value and dignity, but they have distinct roles and functions in the home and in the church. [9]

We are called as women to affirm and encourage men as they seek to express godly masculinity, and to honor and support God-ordained male leadership in the home and in the church. [10]

Marriage, as created by God, is a sacred, binding, lifelong covenant between one man and one woman. [11]

When we respond humbly to male leadership in our homes and churches, we demonstrate a noble submission to authority that reflects Christ's submission to God His Father. [12]

Selfish insistence on personal rights is contrary to the spirit of Christ who humbled Himself, took on the form of a servant, and laid down His life for us. [13]

Human life is precious to God and is to be valued and protected, from the point of conception until rightful death. [14]

Children are a blessing from God; women are uniquely designed to be bearers and nurturers of life, whether it be their own biological or adopted children, or other children in their sphere of influence. [15]

God's plan for gender is wider than marriage; all women, whether married or single, are to model femininity in their various relationships, by exhibiting a distinctive modesty, responsiveness, and gentleness of spirit. [16]

Suffering is an inevitable reality in a fallen world; at times we will be called to suffer for doing what is good—looking to heavenly reward rather than earthly comfort—for the sake of the gospel and the advancement of Christ's Kingdom. [17]

Mature Christian women have a responsibility to leave a legacy of faith, by discipling younger women in the Word and ways of God and modeling for the next generation lives of fruitful femininity. [18]

Believing the above, we declare our desire and intent to be "True Women" of God. *We consecrate ourselves* to fulfill His calling and purposes for our lives. *By His grace and in humble dependence on His power, we will:*

1. Seek to love the Lord our God with all our heart, soul, mind, and strength. [19]

2. Gladly yield control of our lives to Christ as Lord—we will say "Yes, Lord" to the Word and the will of God. [20]

3. Be women of the Word, seeking to grow in our knowledge of Scripture and to live in accord with sound doctrine in every area of our lives. [21]

4. Nurture our fellowship and communion with God through prayer—in praise, thanksgiving, confession, intercession, and supplication. [22]

5. Embrace and express our unique design and calling as women with humility, gratitude, faith, and joy. [23]

6. Seek to glorify God by cultivating such virtues as purity, modesty, submission, meekness, and love. [24]

7. Show proper respect to both men and women, created in the image of God, esteeming others as better than ourselves, seeking to build them up, and putting off bitterness, anger, and evil speaking. [25]

8. Be faithfully engaged in our local church, submitting ourselves to our spiritual leaders, growing in the context of the community of faith, and using the gifts He has given us to serve others, to build up the Body of Christ, and to fulfill His redemptive purposes in the world. [26]

9. Seek to establish homes that manifest the love, grace, beauty, and order of God, that provide a climate conducive to nurturing life, and that extend Christian hospitality to those outside the walls of our homes. [27]

10. Honor the sacredness, purity, and permanence of the marriage covenant—whether ours or others'. [28]

11. Receive children as a blessing from the Lord, seeking to train them to love and follow Christ and to consecrate their lives for the sake of His gospel and Kingdom. [29]

12. Live out the mandate of Titus 2—as older women, modeling godliness and training younger women to be pleasing to God in every respect; as younger women, receiving instruction with meekness and humility and aspiring to become mature women of God who in turn will train the next generation. [30]

13. Seek opportunities to share the gospel of Christ with unbelievers. [31]

14. Reflect God's heart for those who are poor, infirm, oppressed, widows, orphans, and prisoners, by reaching out to minister to their practical and spiritual needs in the name of Christ. [32]

15. Pray for a movement of revival and reformation among God's people that will result in the advancement of the kingdom and gospel of Christ among all nations. [33]

Who knows whether you have

come into the kingdom

for such a time as this?

Esther 4:14 NKJV

Supporting Scriptures

1. 1 Cor. 8:6; Col. 1:16; Rev. 4:11

2. Gen. 1:26-27; 2:18; 1 Cor. 11:8

3. Gen. 3:1-7, 15-16; Mark 1:15; 1 Cor. 15:1-4

4. Prov. 14:12; Jer. 17:9; Rom. 3:18, 8:6-7; 2 Tim. 3:16

5. Eph. 4:22-24; Col. 3:12-14; Titus 2:14

6. Josh. 1:8; 2 Tim. 3:16; 2 Pet. 1:20-21; 3:15-16

7. 1 Tim. 2:9; Tit. 2:3-5; 1 Pet. 3:3-6

8. John 15:1-5; 1 Cor. 15:10; Eph. 2:8-10; Phil. 2:12-13

9. Gen. 1:26-28; 2:18; Gal. 3:26-28; Eph. 5:22-33

10. Mark 9:35; 10:42-45; Gen. 2:18; 1 Pet. 5:1-4; 1 Cor. 14:34; 1 Tim. 2:12-3:7

11. Gen. 2:24; Mark 10:7-9

12. Eph. 5:22-33; 1 Cor. 11:3

13. Luke 13:30; John 15:13; Eph. 4:32; Phil. 2:5-8

14. Ps. 139:13-16

15. Gen 1:28; 9:1; Psalm 127; Tit. 2:4-5

16. 1 Cor. 11:2-16; 1 Tim. 2:9-13

17. Matt. 5:10-12; 2 Cor. 4:17; James 1:12; 1 Pet. 2:21-22; 3:14-17; 4:14

18. Tit. 2:3-5

19. Deut. 6:4-5; Mark 12:29-30

20. Ps. 25:4-5; Rom. 6:11-13; 16-18; Eph. 5:15-17

21. Acts 17:11; 1 Pet. 1:15; 2 Pet. 3:17-18; Titus 2:1, 3-5, 7

22. Psalm 5:2; Phil. 4:6; 1 Tim. 2:1-2

23. Prov. 31:10-31; Col. 3:18; Eph. 5:22-24, 33b

24. Rom. 12:9-21; 1 Pet. 3:1-6; 1 Tim. 2:9-14

25. Eph. 4:29-32; Phil. 2:1-4; James 3:7-10; 4:11

26. Rom. 12:6-8; 14:19; Eph. 4:15, 29; Heb. 13:17

27. Prov. 31:10-31; 1 Tim. 5:10; 1 John 3:17-18

28. Matt. 5:27-28; Mark 10:5-9; 1 Cor. 6:15-20; Heb. 13:4

29. Ps. 127:3; Prov. 4:1-23; 22:6

30. Titus 2:3-5

31. Matt. 28:19-20; Col. 4:3-6

32. Matt. 25:36; Luke 10:25-37; James 1:27; 1 Tim. 6:17-19

33. 2 Chron. 7:14; Ps. 51:1-10; 85:6; 2 Peter 3:9

*N*ow is the time!

I desire to be a part of a countercultural,
spiritual revolution among Christian women in our day.

I have read and personally affirm the True Woman Manifesto,
and I hereby express my desire to join other women in living out and
reproducing its message—to the end that Christ may be exalted
and the glory and redeeming love of God may be
displayed throughout the whole earth.

_____

NAME   DATE

Go to www.TrueWoman.com/Manifesto to add
your signature to the True Woman Manifesto.

NOTES

Introduction: Designer Womanhood

1. Susan Hunt, *By Design: God's Distinctive Calling for Women* (Franklin, TN: Legacy Communications, 1994), 17.

2. One of the key influences the Lord used to birth a burden for a countercultural revolution in my (Nancy's) heart was a book by Mary, originally titled *The Feminist Gospel*, since reprinted as *The Feminist Mistake* (Crossway, 2005). This eye-opening book, which I first read in 1997, helped me understand how the feminist movement had penetrated and permeated not only our culture, but even our churches. It planted the seeds for much of what God is doing through the True Woman movement today.

3. Elisabeth Elliot, *Let Me Be a Woman* (Carol Stream, IL: Tyndale House, 1976), 52.

Week One: Gender Matters

1. *Biblical Foundations for Manhood and Womanhood*, ed. by Wayne Grudem (Foundations for the Family Series), (Wheaton, IL: Crossway Books, 2002), 20.

Week Two: Snips and Snails

1. www.people.com/people/videos/0,,20396440,00.html.

2. John Piper, *What's the Difference? Manhood and Womanhood Defined according to the Bible* (Wheaton, IL: Crossway Books, 1990), 16.

3. Ibid., 16–17.

4. Ibid., 23.

Week Three: Sugar and Spice

1. Elisabeth Elliot, *Let Me Be a Woman* (Carol Stream, IL: Tyndale House, 1976), 61.

2. For more information about physical and hormonal differences between men and women:

    www.steadyhealth.com/articles/Difference_between_male_and_female_structures__mental_and_physical__a613.html

    http://blisstree.com/feel/5-physical-differences-between-women-and-men/

    http://library.enlisted.info/field-manuals/series-2/FM21_20/APPA.PDF

    www.medicaleducationonline.org/index.php?option=com_content&task=view&id=46&Itemid=69

    www.narth.com/docs/york.html

    www.enotes.com/male-female-article

    www.sciencedaily.com/releases/2009/03/090302115755.htm

    www.bloomingbellys.com/bb-blog/pain-in-labour-your-hormones-are-your-helpers/http://healthguide.howstuffworks.com/estrogen-and-testosterone-hormones-dictionary.htm

3. Francis Brown, Samuel Rolles Driver, Charles Augustus Briggs, *Enhanced Brown-Driver-Briggs Hebrew and English Lexicon*, electronic ed. Oak Harbor, WA: Logos Research Systems, 2000, S. 61.

    Also, R. Laird Harris, Gleason L. Archer, Bruce K. Waltke :*Theological Wordbook of the Old Testament*, electronic ed. Chicago: Moody, 1999, c1980, S. 059.

    Also, John McArthur sermon: http://www.biblebb.com/files/mac/90-228.htm.

4. See references in chapter 3, endnote 2.

5. John Piper, *What's the Difference? Manhood and Womanhood Defined according to the Bible* (Wheaton, IL: Crossway Books, 1990), 49–50.

Week Five: Battle of the Sexes

1. Raymond C. Ortlund Jr., *Recovering Biblical Manhood & Womanhood: A Response to Evangelical Feminism* (Wheaton, IL: Crossway, 1999), 95.

2. www.telegraph.co.uk/news/worldnews/europe/austria/1922110/Austria-The-horror-of-being-Frau-Fritzl.html; also, marriage.about.com/od/infamous/a/fritzljosef.htm; also, telegraph.co.uk/news/newstopics/joseffritzl/4991077/Josef-Fritzl-trial-profile-of-a-monster.html.

3. Mary Kassian, *The Feminist Mistake* (Wheaton: Crossway, 2005), 72.

4. Betty Friedan, *"It Changed My Life": Writings on the Women's Movement—with a new introduction*; originally published by (New York: Random House, 1976). First Harvard University Press paperback edition, 1998, xvi .

5. http://womenshistory.about.com/od/quotes/a/de_beauvoir_2.htm.

6. Mary Daly, *Beyond God the Father: Toward a Philosophy of Women's Liberation* (Boston: Beacon Press, 1973), 8.

7. Germaine Greer, *The Female Eunuch* (London: Paladin Grafton Books, 1970), 115.

8. The passage does not specify what kind of animal the Lord sacrificed, but based on the sacrificial system of the Old Testament and the symbolism of Jesus as the "Lamb of God," it is quite probable that the animal was a lamb.

Week Six: Hear Me Roar

1. Marcia Cohen, *The Sisterhood: The Inside Story of the Women's Movement and the Leaders Who Made It Happen* (New York: Ballantine Books, division of Random House, 1988), 286.

2. www. prnewswire.com/news-releases/newsweek-cover-the-girls-gone-wild-effect-54272887.html.

3. www.enlightennext.org/magazine/j37/pornutopia.asp.

4. Ibid.

5. Jennifer Baumgardner and Amy Richards, *Manifesta: Young Women, Feminism, and the Future*; 10th Anniversary Edition (New York: Farrar, Straus and Giroux, 2010), 103.

6. www.maureenmullarkey.com/essays/dinnerparty.html. See also www.brooklynmuseum.org/eascfa/.

7. Nancy Gibbs, "What Women Want Now," *Time,* Oct 14, 2009, www.time.com/time/specials/packages/article/0,28804,1930277_1930145_1930309,00.html

   See also Betsey Stevenson and Justin Wolfers, "The Paradox of Declining Female Happiness," http://bpp.wharton.upenn.edu/betseys/papers/Paradox%20of%20declining%20female%20happiness.pdf.

Week Seven: Total Makeover

1. Amy Carmichael, *Gold Cord: The Story of a Fellowship* (Fort Washington, PA: Christian Literature Crusade, 1999), 57.

2. John MacArthur, MacArthur New Testament Commentary, *Titus* (Chicago: Moody, 1996), 88.

3. www.ywca.org/atf/cf/%7B3B450FA5-108B-4D2E-B3D0-C31487243E6A%7D/Beauty%20at%20Any%20Cost.pdf.

4. C. S. Lewis, *The Weight of Glory* (1941) chap. 1, para. 1. (pp. 3–4) as quoted in "The Quotable Lewis: An encyclopedic selection of quotes from the complete published works of C. S. Lewis, ed. Wayne Martindale and Jerry Root (Wheaton, IL: Tyndale, 1989), 352 .

Week Eight: Sisterhood Is Powerful

1. G. J. Wenham (2002) *Vol. 1: Word Biblical Commentary: Genesis 1–15*. Word Biblical Commentary (68). Dallas: Word, Incorporated. Comment on Genesis 2:18. Electronic Edition.

2. Betty Friedan, *The Feminine Mystique*, Twentieth Anniversary Edition (New York: Dell Publishing, 1983), 11.

3. "Where She Is and Where She's Going," *Time*, March 20, 1972, www.time.com/time/magazine/article/0,9171,942510,00.html.

4. See David Leonhardt, "Why are men happier than women?", *New York Times*, September 25, 2007, http://www.nytimes.com/2007/09/25/business/worldbusiness/25iht-leonhardt.7636350.html;

   Also, Maureen Dowd, "Blue Is the New Black," *New York Times*, September 19, 2009, www.nytimes.com/2009/09/20/opinion/20dowd.html; also, CNN video: www.momversation.com/articles/women-less-happy-men.

5. Susan Hunt and Barbara Thompson, *The Legacy of Biblical Womanhood* (Wheaton, IL: Crossway Books, 2003),12.

6. Susan Hunt, *Spiritual Mothering: The Titus 2 Model for Women Mentoring Women* (Wheaton, IL: Crossway Books, 1992), 12.

7. John Angell James, *Female Piety: The Young Woman's Friend and Guide through Life to Immortality* (Morgan, PA: Soli Deo Gloria, 1995), 72.

8. Ibid., 72–73.

Afterword: Different By Design

1. Analogy taken from *Girls Gone Wise*, by Mary Kassian (Chicago: Moody, 2010), 185.

Heartfelt Thanks . . .

We are both blessed to be surrounded and supported by a host of like-minded, servant-hearted friends and colleagues, apart from whose encouragement, help, and prayers undertakings such as this resource would never come to fruition.

Of the many who played a part in the birthing of *True Woman 101*, special gratitude is due to:

Greg Thornton and *Holly Kisly*, along with our other friends at *Moody Publishers*, whose partnership with us goes deeper and further than most will ever know.

Mike Neises, who oversees *Revive Our Hearts* publishing efforts, and who in this project has successfully and graciously managed to manage not one but two authors (who happen to live in two different countries).

Martin Jones, *Sandy Bixel*, and *Jessie Stoltzfus*—the administrative team that in countless ways, large and small, mostly unseen and unsung, helps keep my (Nancy's) head (and heart) above water when I am in the throes of a major project.

Brent Kassian, who is my (Mary's) sounding board. He helps me process ideas, clarify concepts, stay focused on what's important, and retain a sense of humor about it all.

Dawn Wilson for providing research assistance and, along with *Paula Hendricks*, valuable "reader input" on early stages of the manuscript.

Dr. Bruce Ware, professor of Christian theology at The Southern Baptist Theological Seminary, for input on the theological questions and issues as they arose, as well as your review of scores of passages in the book. So grateful for your help once again!

Dr. Peter Gentry and *Dr. Robert Plummer*, also of The Southern Baptist Theological Seminary, for their review of references to Hebrew and Greek words and concepts (facilitated by our mutual friend, Jennifer Lyell).

Our dear *Praying Friends*—He knows your names—who faithfully lifted us up to the throne of grace throughout this many-month journey. The prayers you have sown on our behalf will reap a great harvest of righteousness for generations to come.

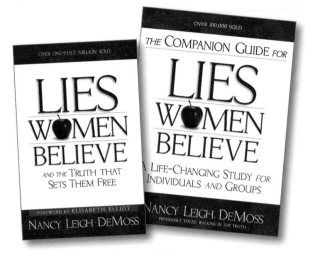

lies women believe

More resources for you, women's study, or teen study

Resources to hand out

- *Free From Lies* —25-pack of leaflets
- *The Truth That Sets Us Free*—25-pack of bookmarks

Lies Women Believe & Companion Guide

- DVD
- Audio book
- Available in Spanish

Lies Young Women Believe & Companion Guide

- *Lies Young Women Believe—Conversation with Dannah*
- CDs
- Audio book
- Available in Spanish

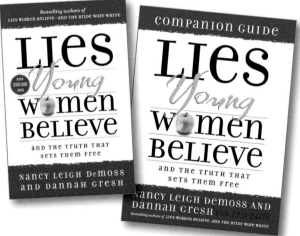

To place your order visit us online at www.ReviveOurHearts.com

Brought to you by:

More resources for Girls Gone Wise!

You'll find videos, a forum, and many other resources to help you learn how to walk wisely on the GirlsGoneWise.com website. And make sure to follow Girls Gone Wise on Facebook (facebook.com/girlgonewise) and Twitter (twitter.com/girlsgonewise) too!

**Also available, *Girls Gone Wise* gear! Get
the bag, mug, and buttons.**

 MOODY
PUBLISHERS

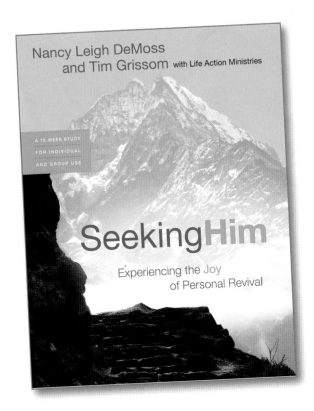

Nancy Leigh DeMoss and Tim Grissom with Life Action Ministries

A 12-WEEK STUDY FOR INDIVIDUAL AND GROUP USE

SeekingHim

Experiencing the Joy of Personal Revival

seeking him

Other resources for you and your ministry

- Church Package
- Small Group Package
- *SeekingHim* Women's DVD Series
- *SeekingHim* Devotions and Prayers 2 CD Set
- Pastor's Resource Kit
- Facilitator's Guide

To place your order visit us online at www.SeekingHim.com

Brought to you by:

 Revive Our Hearts | MOODY PUBLISHERS | LIFE ACTION Revival Ministries